WORK WITH I

BRIAN WILLIAMS

Published by
VENTURE PRESS
16 Kent Street
Birmingham
B5 6RD
Tel: 021 622 3911

First Published 1991

British Library Cataloguing in Publication Data

Williams, Brian
Work with Prisoners.
I. Title
943.086

ISBN 0 900 102 942 (paperback)

To my Father and the memory of my Mother

CONTENTS

ACKNOWLEDGEMENTS

Throughout the book, use is made of unpublished interviews with prisoners and professionals. The interviews were carried out on the understanding that the identity of the informants would not be disclosed, and the material is not therefore attributed. It cannot go unacknowledged, however, and I would like to thank everyone who patiently endured my questions for their time and their consideration of sometimes painful subjects. If this book improves our future work with prisoners, it will have been worth their while.

In addition to the prisoners who must obviously remain anonymous, many people have helped with the research for the book. It would not be possible to name them all, but I would like to thank all who gave advice, helped with research and checked drafts; Una Padel, Ellie Roy, Jim McManus, Ruth Hopkins, Peter Tarleton and the Chaplaincy staff at Lindholme Prison, Chris Needham and especially Peter Clark . Andrew Willis guided me in the study which led me to write the book. Practical help was received from Teesside Polytechnic research committee and many of its library staff, particularly Alma Cuthbertson, and from Sally Arkley at Venture Press. Considerable encouragement was received from Andrew Shephard, Jo Campling, the late John Pendleton and Barbara Prescott. I owe them all my thanks.

Introduction

This book is intended mainly for probation officers and social workers, as a basic handbook on how to work with prisoners. It is also likely to be of use to other caring professionals working with prisoners, both those who do so regularly and those for whom contact with prisons and prisoners is comparatively rare. It is also designed to be used by voluntary workers.

Prisons are large, sophisticated bureaucracies. This makes it hard for those new to them, and those hostile to their aims, to work with them. No matter how much we disapprove of the prison system and what it does to people, it is a fact of life, and it holds large numbers of inmates who need outside contacts and help. It is easier to give this help if one has some basic knowledge about how prisons work and what the people working in them do.

Prisons also have a culture of their own, partly secret, but much-researched. It helps to have some knowledge of this before talking to prisoners or to people who work in prisons. With prisoners and staff, one's credibility is enhanced by showing that one knows something of what it is like to be in their position. In recent years, work has begun on finding out from a 'consumer' perspective what the clients of social work think and feel about the service they get. This is in its infancy so far as prisoners are concerned, but some work has been done and it is reviewed briefly in Chapters One and Five.

Oddly, nobody has written a book about social work with prisoners since Mark Monger's *Casework in After-Care*(1967). Good though it was, Monger's book is now seriously out of date. The prisons and the Probation Service have changed enormously in the intervening quarter century, and so have attitudes to prisoners and government policies about them. The number of life sentence prisoners has vastly increased, the prison system has grown and grown, and new problems like the increasing use of drugs and the spread of AIDS have arrived. During the same period, some positive changes have also occurred: prisons are less secretive places than they were, prisoners have successfully taken action to improve their legal rights, the understanding of the harmful effects

1

of imprisonment has increased, and services for prisoners have improved in certain areas (particularly because of self-help groups). The emphasis in working with prisoners has shifted from giving them psychological insights to finding out what practical help they want.

Most profound of all has been the impact of the seemingly permanent crisis the prison system in this country has been in for decades. The prisons have been overcrowded, sometimes explosive and unpredictable places for as long as many of the people in them can remember. It was not always so, and this is apparent to anyone who reads Monger's book today. There was time and privacy then for probation officers to engage in therapeutic casework with prisoners. Apart from long-term prisoners in dispersal (and some in training) prisons, adult prisoners have to cope in a crisis-ridden system. They are constantly aware of this; when they are locked up for long hours because staff are not available to escort them to work or classes, when they have to use a chamber pot at night, when they are suddenly moved from one prison to another without notice, when they get caught up in violence and disorder. People trying to work with prisoners are also constantly reminded of the crisis and of the ways in which it is being managed. Prison staff who want to see inmates may not be able to do so if they are in segregation, or if the prison officers are having a union meeting. Education officers may find students disappearing, or classes being cancelled altogether, due to staff problems. Outsiders find their visits limited to the minimum time, in crowded visiting areas often without facilities for children, or they may even arrive at the prison to find that their client or loved one has been moved without anyone being told.

Some of these areas are considered in what follows. Where space does not allow much detail, further reading is recommended. Wherever possible, prisoners' own views are considered.

Chapter One looks at probation officers' work with prisoners, and the historical and political reasons for its neglect. It also suggests that such work can nevertheless be effective, but that prisoners themselves tend to be rather cynical about this.

Chapter Two is concerned with what it is like to be in prison. There is a rich source of information in prisoners' own writings, and these are reviewed, along with psychological and criminological material. The implications for prisoners' families, friends and advisers are considered, as are the specific difficulties faced by women and black people in prison.

In Chapter Three, the work of the various people who provide services for prisoners is reviewed. Where possible, members of the occupational groups concerned have been interviewed to ensure that the descriptions of their work are accurate. The importance of liaison between the different groups is emphasised, and some of the problems arising from the involvement of professional people in the welfare of prisoners are pointed out. The particular difficulties faced by women and black people working in prison or with prisoners are considered, along with the formal and other mechanisms for tackling racism in prisons.

The title of Chapter Four speaks for itself: it is about how to work with prisoners, looking in some detail at questions like making best use of different types of contact with prisoners (by letter, phone and visits). There is a discussion of how to break bad news to people in prison, and how to help them cope with their stress and fears. Some specific areas where groups of prisoners are badly served by the existing system are examined.

Chapter Five then reviews what is known about prisoners' own views on some of the topics already covered. How can we offer prisoners a better service, within the existing constraints? What needs to be changed, and how? The chapter also includes a summary of the ways of working effectively with prisoners described earlier.

Finally, there is a selective and critical list of recommended articles and books. Some of the most important organisations working with prisoners are briefly described, with a summary of the services they offer.

Because the situation of women prisoners is so very distinctive in this country, and because women are in such a minority in the prison population, most of the book is about male prisoners. Where possible, the distinctiveness of female prisoners' experience is acknowledged in the text, but it would be untrue to assert that in this matter the use of 'he' is simply a convention. Not everything written here about male prisoners applies to women. There are important differences in working with women prisoners, and appropriate further reading is recommended for those needing more information about this.

1. Working with Prisoners: The Cinderella Service

The history of welfare work with prisoners makes it easy to see why this work has been neglected, even though more intensive work might prove worthwhile. In a way, neglecting to engage with people in prison has made it more difficult to work with them: prisoners do not feel particularly well-disposed towards people who suddenly start to show an interest in their welfare towards the end of their sentences, and the belief that the potential helping agencies do not care has a chance to become entrenched during the earlier period of little contact.

Outside agencies first began to work with prisoners from charitable and religious motives. This meant that services were always provided on a discretionary basis, rather than of right. For various reasons, political and professional, this tendency has continued, leading to the status of work with prisoners as the 'Cinderella' left behind when other kinds of welfare work were allocated greater resources. Recent government policy towards the Probation Service has strengthened this trend, and for their own reasons, the prison officers' and probation officers' unions have also continued it.

As Frank Dawtry put it, writing about voluntary after-care work by the Probation Service, 'After-care is in fact the 'Cinderella' of every service concerned with the treatment of offenders and consequently it has never yet been properly and efficiently organised' (Dawtry, 1963).

The Reasons for the Neglect of Work with Prisoners

Work with prisoners on their release had its origins in philanthropic efforts by people whose main interest was in other areas of work. Early initiatives , for example, were made by Prison Gate Missions which offered food, cash and help with accommodation - but only to those who were susceptible to the

5

Christian message the Missions mainly existed to propagate, and prepared to consider signing a 'pledge' to give up drinking. Prior to this, the only help available to prisoners on release was in those areas which had Discharged Prisoners' Aid Societies, or where magistrates decided to use their power to assist them . Such help was given, like all charity at that time, cautiously, in the belief that excessive generosity would undermine the self-sufficiency of the poor. In practice, this meant that it was usually given in a grudging and degrading manner.

This concern to give help only to the 'deserving poor' lived on into the twentieth century, and helped to shape attitudes to after-care.

Similar considerations have influenced the provision of throughcare - the notion that care for prisoners' welfare needs to begin during their sentence and not just at the end of it. The Borstal system for young offenders (a form of imprisonment based on the ethos of the public schools, whose stated aim was to provide facilities for young offenders in custody which would give them a chance of rehabilitation by training them for a trade) had throughcare as one of its central characteristics. However, help after release was provided by Police Court Missionaries (and later by their successors, field probation officers) who received no recognition for the work (Bochel, 1976).

If provision for statutory supervision was introduced so slowly and in such a piecemeal way (many areas did not have a local Police Court Missionary, and the Probation Service was thin on the ground until at least the 1940s (Jarvis, 1972)), it is clear that voluntary aftercare was even more neglected. 'Voluntary' here refers to the client, but one might be forgiven for thinking that providing aftercare was voluntary for probation officers. This distinction has continued to be made up to this day, and prisoners serving short-term sentences need not be offered any assistance by the Probation Service once they are discharged. It has been argued that this is a false economy, since the clients being targeted for priority by the Probation Service in preference to providing voluntary after-care are often the same people at a slightly different stage in their criminal careers (Hicks, in NAPO, 1986). The danger is that relatively minor offenders get caught in the 'revolving door' of offending related to drink, serving repeated sentences or spending time in hospital after committing trivial thefts.

The provision of welfare assistance to prisoners from inside the institutions was as piecemeal in its development as services for ex-prisoners. When the emphasis of aftercare changed from aid-on-discharge to individual casework in the mid-1950s, the role of Aid Society agents working in prisons changed, and they became Prison Welfare Officers. Many of the same people occupied these posts, however, and some of them remained in post when the Probation Service took over the work in 1966. It was thus a long process for probation officers to become recognised as social workers with offenders, rather than welfare administrators, and even now, many prison officers speak of 'the Welfare'. Particularly in local prisons, probation officers are too busy to engage with many prisoners in work in any depth, and researchers on behalf of NACRO noted that 'often the natural responses of the prison welfare officers to their impossible situation were interpreted by inmates as cynicism or lack of interest' (Irving & Priestley, 1970).

Probation officers in prisons developed - or continued to use - screening devices common to 'street-level bureaucrats' everywhere, to try and reduce the demands made upon their time, and thus justified the cynical and wary attitudes of many prisoners towards them.

Those who have been concerned with the provision of welfare assistance to prisoners on a statutory basis have also tended to give the work low priority, although most Probation Services at least nominally give this work a high priority (Williams, 1990). High priority in policy documents is not necessarily translated into individual workers' practice, though, and there are many ways in which slippage can occur between the two. There is the 'implementation gap' between any central policy-making and practice at ground level. In the present case, this is complicated by the autonomy allowed to individual probation officers. Their practice is idiosyncratic, and they tend to make policy incrementally: it may not be their deliberate intention to neglect those of their clients who are in custody, but by consistently doing so they make this a policy. It is always easier, when under pressure, to work with the clients who present themselves in person to remind one of their demands. Rationing devices such as postponing or cancelling visits to prisoners emerge as coping mechanisms for street-level bureaucrats (Lipsky, 1980; Howe, 1986).

Autobiographical accounts by ex-prisoners and research on prisoners' views on throughcare paint a consistent picture of half-hearted offers of help on release (Peckham, 1985; Boyle, 1984; Kingston, 1979). It has been agreed since the 1960s that aftercare is unlikely to succeed if some sort of relationship was not built during the prisoner's sentence (Parris, 1968; Pearce, 1969; Monger, 1967), for obvious reasons:

> After-care, it is suggested, is a misnomer which has been literally interpreted and which has done far more harm than good. To the offender, any would-be helper who arrives on the scene after sentence is all over, arrives at precisely the time when he wants help least (Monger et al, 1981).

Prisoners resent it when, as often happens, probation officers contact them for the first time when parole reports are requested. Not surprisingly, they tend to feel that probation officers ought to get to know them before trying to write such reports.

The overall picture, then, is of a history of low priority being given to welfare work with prisoners, in the context of paternalistic services which were intended mainly for other purposes than the welfare of individual prisoners. Field probation officers, in particular, have been encouraged to give priority to work which keeps people out of custody, and the Home Office 1984 Statement of National Objectives and Priorities made it clear that this meant court reports, probation and community service orders rather than throughcare. The trend has been stronger in recent years, with the emergence of proposals to privatise aftercare work and further concentrate resources upon community disposals and court reports (Home Office, 1990).

The emergence of shared work between prison officers and probation officers has, paradoxically, made matters worse. The Prison Officers' Association passed a resolution at its 1963 annual conference calling for a greater role in rehabilitation and after-care for uniformed staff.

The outcome was the establishment of a working party which met Home Office officials to discuss increasing prison officers' welfare role. It continued to meet until it was eventually disbanded in 1981, and 'it never got anywhere' (Stern, 1987). That the Association should take such a far-reaching decision, but nothing should come of it for so long, suggests that there was a rhetorical element in its claim that a greater role in rehabilitation was what prison officers wanted. Arguably, this allowed negotiators to claim that prison officers' role was changing and that new skills were needed, when they discussed their salaries with the employers. The decision also arose from a desire to improve the image of professionalism of prison officers, who had for so long been regarded as mere turnkeys.

However, the policy was taken seriously in some areas. By the 1980s, experiments in shared working had begun, with the encouragement of the Home Office, although many prison officers were sceptical about their value.

Nevertheless, by 1987 there was a significant number of shared working schemes, mainly in the dispersal and training prisons where the regimes are relatively relaxed and the inmate population more stable than in the local prisons. By that time, the POA was again highlighting the advantages of shared work. Its Vice-Chair expressed the view at a conference in 1986 that 'Involvement in welfare would enhance the role of the prison officer which had become devalued' (reported in NAPO, 1986). It is clear today that shared throughcare work between prison and probation officers is a matter of 'public policy', as evidenced by Circular Instructions on the subject, even if implementation of the policy is patchy and it is not working well in some areas (Chief Inspector, 1989).

A parallel development was the decision by the annual conference of the National Association of Probation Officers in 1981 that 'social work help to prisoners would be provided most effectively by withdrawing seconded probation officers from prisons, and by the Probation Service as a whole taking on the responsibility of working with prisoners' (NAPO, 1987). Debate about this issue had gone on within the Association for 15 years, beginning with support for joint working from 1971. Negotiations began with the Prison Officers' Association in an attempt to safeguard the interests of probation officers working in prisons, and agreement was reached about this in 1984.

The main argument for probation officers' withdrawal was that they did not succeed in changing the prisons from within, the strategy that they had previously decided to pursue, and that their presence led to them taking on institutional duties and values, which did nothing to help their clients. In the document later produced as part of the campaign for the policy, other reasons were also given; the involvement of prison officers in welfare work would make them more aware of prisoners' needs, joint working had not freed prison-based probation officers from 'welfare' tasks, and these humble duties could just as well be performed by prison officers ('the need to hand over to other people some of the less skilled tasks which is loosely called welfare work' - NAPO, 1987). The review by Jepson and Elliott of the prison probation officer's role, published in 1984, was called in aid of the latter argument, but their findings were oversimplified in the NAPO document.

In any event, prison-based probation officers became more open about their wish to discard the low-status 'welfare' work in favour of more rewarding tasks suited to their skills and training, including the selection and training of 'welfare' prison officers, research and monitoring, group-work with prisoners with specific needs, and involvement in the management of the prisons.

The danger of this is that probation officers in prisons spend less time in routine contacts with prisoners which might reveal needs deeper than the presenting problem (the 'welfare' request): if the prisoners never meet probation officers, they are unlikely to think of them as a source of help. Many prisoners are extremely sceptical about the motives and qualifications of uniformed staff engaged in welfare work, and a significant minority refuse to use such a service, cutting themselves off from the welfare service . In their anxiety to carve out a more rewarding and professional task, probation officers may be hastening the day when there is no need for them to work with prisoners at all.

To summarise, throughcare work has historically been discretionary - and therefore seen as dispensable - and provided in a paternalistic manner which made it unattractive to potential clients. In recent years, government financial priorities have led to greater emphasis being placed upon work outside , using resources which might otherwise have been provided for less politically popular areas of work including throughcare. In all this, the quest for professional status by prison officers and probation officers has led to further downgrading of throughcare as an area of work. There is considerable wariness in the relationship between the prison and probation officers' trade unions, and also in the attitude of both towards the voluntary agencies which might be interested in taking on throughcare work if it were to be privatised on a larger scale than has so far occurred (see Home Office, 1990). These uneasy relationships make it unlikely that the prison officers,the probation officers and the voluntary organisations (in combination, potentially a powerful lobby for change) will trust each other enough to cooperate in defence of existing throughcare arrangements.

Evidence about the Effectiveness of Work with Prisoners

The results of most of the systematic studies of the effectiveness of work with prisoners have been highly ambiguous. Ambitious attempts were made to show that intensive probation work with prisoners was effective, but the results were inconclusive. These studies were published at a time when there was a loss of confidence about the effectiveness of probation work generally, and they tended to be incorporated into the general atmosphere of 'nothing works' (See Raynor, 1985, for a fuller account).

Early in the involvement of the Probation Service in prison social work, Margaret Shaw headed a team which carried out an expensive and ambitious experimental research project in four Midlands prisons. Additional probation staff were provided, so that the impact of intensive work with long-term prisoners could be compared with the normal level of throughcare involvement. Certain types of offender were found to be less likely to reoffend within a set period of release, if they had intensive attention from the prison probation officer. Shaw's study was one of three, but the other two were never completed.

An experiment of a different kind was undertaken by Hollows and Wood, who took advantage of the fact that there had been no social worker in a Scottish prison for three years, and studied the stop-gap arrangements which evolved. Uniformed staff developed groupwork and individual welfare services in collaboration with outside agencies, although they found that they could not engage field social workers in many cases. But an effective alternative to prison-based social work services could perhaps have been developed if uniformed staff were involved fully and if they were given appropriate training. Further research would be needed before these suggestions could be proved or disproved at all decisively (Hollows & Wood, 1983).

In one study where prisoners were asked for their views about the usefulness of the service provided by probation officers, their reaction to the help they received with immediate 'welfare' problems was generally favourable, but in another the prisoners did not see the services given as predominantly helpful (Holborn, 1975 and Corden et al, 1980). It has been suggested in two studies that systematic throughcare work with prisoners is the exception rather than the rule (Craig, 1984; Williams, 1990). Certainly, when the outcomes of work with individual prisoners were studied, it was clear that socially isolated short-term prisoners were on average in worse accommodation after release than before they were imprisoned, and more of them were homeless (Corden et al, 1979).

Given this lack of evidence for the effectiveness of throughcare, one might be tempted to conclude that it is a waste of time. It would be more scientific, however, to say that the case is so far not proven either way. The traditional criminological measure of effectiveness - reconviction rates - is in any case of dubious value when we come to look at people in prison. Whatever is done with them, they have a high probability of reconviction simply because they are in prison. Drawing, therefore, on 'softer' forms of evidence, the next section looks briefly at the views of some prisoners as to whether they find throughcare helpful or valuable. There is also some interesting material in the form of subjective expressions of opinion by probation officers. Echoing the views of John Hicks, quoted above, another probation officer has written, 'If the Service is committed to working with those most at risk of custody then reconviction figures clearly indicate that it should be focusing its attention on those currently in prison' (Raban, 1987).

The potential value of throughcare being given a higher priority is clearly recognised in some quarters at least in the Probation Service.

As we have seen, though, most probation officers do not seem to give a very high priority to their throughcare work in practice, although this is less true of high-profile statutory work with lifers, where the Probation Service has much higher standards of accountability and monitoring . Prison-based probation officers, however, seem to return to field-work with a changed view of throughcare, and to treat it as a much higher priority. Most probation officers who work in prisons are concerned to shed what they see as frustrating and time-wasting 'welfare' type work, in order to concentrate upon working in greater depth with some of their potentially huge caseload of clients. Nevertheless, they do see the importance of these mundane tasks, not only in cementing trusting relationships with prisoners, but in relieving anxiety and mitigating the effects of imprisonment   They are not suggesting that nobody should help prisoners with these problems, but rather that it does not require sophisticated training to deal with them.

Less routine tasks include group work, often done jointly with other professionals like education officers, psychologists, chaplains and prison officers. Groups look at particular types of offending, and at social problems experienced by prisoners. Again, there seems to be a consensus that such work is important, although in practice it may emerge only in bemoaning that there is no time to do it! Those who do become involved in such work report upon it enthusiastically.

The minority of field probation officers who engage in more than routine or haphazard work with prisoners seem to find their involvement fulfilling, and they speak of some successes. In the last analysis, however, the subjective views of the prisoners on the receiving end of their services are of more interest than whether probation officers find this work satisfying (e.g. Cowburn, 1989).

Prisoners' Attitudes to Outside Help

Not surprisingly, the majority of prisoners prefer to feel self-reliant, and would rather go to their families and friends for help than approach any official agency. Many regard the welfare services as provided for the use of 'inadequates' - although they call upon the services themselves at times of crisis (Williams, 1991).

Much depends, of course, upon their attitudes to the agencies concerned at the time of their sentence. People who are active members of a religious congregation would seem to be more likely to want to make use of the services of the chaplaincy than those who are not. Men with a positive view of their field probation officer, whether arising from the preparation of a court report or from a previous period of probation, are more likely to feel positively about using the services of prison probation officers.

Not very much work has been done to establish the views of prisoners about the service they receive from the different caring professions during their sentences. What evidence there is, suggests that the systematic neglect of work with prisoners is reflected in a correspondingly negative attitude of many potential clients towards the Probation Service.

Those prisoners who have written about their experiences are not, of course, necessarily representative of the prison population at large, in the sense that many of them are either notorious for their offences, or sufficiently literate to wish and be able to tell their own stories - or both. This does not necessarily invalidate the information they give, however (Davies, 1974). Perhaps prison autobiographies are unrepresentative in some respects, but the overriding impression they give of all the caring professionals is difficult to ignore: they come across as peripheral to the main concerns of prisoners (except for chaplains in the case of some explicitly religious accounts of conversion in prison). A survey of this literature offers little comfort to chaplains, probation officers or psychologists trying to justify their positions in the prisons, because their impact on individual prisoners seems generally to be marginal:

> The overall effect of reading prisoners' autobiographies is a very depressing one, and this applies at least as much to the area of welfare and after-care where one can perhaps recognise that there are good intentions on the part of those in authority (Davies, 1974).

In autobiographies, where the consumer selects the topics to be covered, the welfare services do not loom large, and what is said about them is largely uncomplimentary. This is not the place for a full survey, but let us look briefly at a selection of comments made in recent years in prisoners' writings about probation officers.

Insofar as attitudes to throughcare are concerned, recent writings by prisoners do contain a range of opinions. But in some respects, there is disturbing consensus.

Prisoners, like other groups of people receiving services from caring professions, are well able to distinguish between the constraints imposed by agencies or by the institution, and difficulties in service delivery caused by personal failings on the part of the worker: like anyone else, prisoners value genuineness. It is not conducive to a good relationship with a prisoner to trot out lame excuses for not being in regular contact, or for not carrying out tasks agreed previously. Yet a high proportion of letters from field probation officers begin with apologies for just such neglect - which may lead to cynicism on prisoners' part. One wrote:

> I would like to say just how little the Probation Service can do to help a man like me. No matter how willing a probation officer is, they are so busy and so tied up with red tape that it is a wonder they ever find time to talk to you. . . . Welfare in prisons is practically non-existent. There are Welfare Officers but they are so over-worked and bound by red tape it is made impossible for them to help you (Fletcher, 1972).

As we have seen, joint working has developed as an attempt to deal with the problem Fletcher identified, but it may lead to a failure to engage with some prisoners at all.

Despite these reservations, prisoners do welcome the interest of a sympathetic and detached outsider, and some see probation officers in this role. Probation officers are seen as people who can be trusted with confidential information - perhaps more so than some of the other professionals working in the prison setting although there is a realistic awareness of the limits of such confidentiality (Williams, 1990). Because it is hard to trust other inmates and staff with intimate information, the prison-based probation officer may be treated as an outsider in this way:

> the majority of things in here you can sort out yourself,
> but y'know, if there's times you need to have a break and
> talk to someone who's outside the prison and outside like
> the cons, it's, y'know, he's handy to have a chat with.

Had prisoners been interviewed about the work of chaplains and psychologists, some would no doubt have given similar replies. Pointing to some of the anxieties discussed in Chapter Two, the prisoners interviewed also mentioned the need to maintain interest in the outside world as part of their battle against becoming institutionalised, and said that it was helpful to have an outside probation officer keeping an eye on their interests at times during the sentence when they became too depressed and inward-looking to do so themselves.

There is, however, an ambivalence on the part of many inmates about the trustworthiness of anyone employed by the prison or by the criminal justice system which imprisoned them. All staff concerned with the welfare of prisoners need to bear in mind that they represent this face of authority, and that they will have a long way to go before they can gain the trust of prisoners. As one friendly interviewee put it:

> I know a lot of other prisoners,...their attitude is, oh sod
> 'em, we don't want to talk to them [probation officers].
> They're treated as y'know, like, officers and policemen
> and society in general. But erm, I try not to think of it that
> way [laughing].

Many prisoners see all prison staff as bureaucrats, simply earning a living. Unkept promises are remembered and held against them. The failure to inform prisoners of their rights (not only by uniformed staff, but by many welfare professionals too: see Chapter Five) is seen as a control mechanism, even when it results from neglect rather than malice. There is sometimes a feeling that discussions about their offending and their lives outside will simply cause time to drag and lead to their doing 'heavy bird'. As we saw earlier in this chapter, a large minority of prisoners also see the welfare services as primarily provided for the use of 'inadequates', and prefer to subscribe to the prevailing subculture which dictates that they use their own resources to deal with their own problems.

Understandably, then, there is considerable ambivalence on the part of prisoners about contact with the caring professions. This needs to be taken into account when we begin work with new clients who are in custody, as does their understandable resentment of authority which makes it hard for prisoners to express positive feelings about any official agency.

In what follows, further use will be made of research findings and prisoners' own accounts, in defining good practice in working with people in prison.

2. The Pains of Imprisonment

Suffering is one very long moment. We cannot divide it by seasons. We can only record its moods, and chronicle their return. With us time itself does not progress. It revolves. It seems to circle round one centre of pain. This immobile quality, which makes each dreadful day in the minutest detail like its brother, seems to communicate itself to those external forces, the very essence of whose existence is ceaseless change. Of seed-time or harvest, of the reapers bending over the corn, or the grape gatherers threading through the vines, of the grass in the orchard made white with broken blossoms or strewn with fallen fruit: of these we know nothing, and can know nothing. - Oscar Wilde, *De Profundis*.

The aim of this chapter is to describe, wherever possible in the words of prisoners themselves, what it is like to be in prison.

There can be few people with any imagination who have not wondered how they would cope with a prison sentence. Those who work with prisoners need to use this imagination constructively, combined with whatever experience they have or know of, to help prisoners to cope. Despite the pain, deprivations and indignities of prison, autobiographies show that prisoners do cope, often in imaginative and dignified ways. The prison culture may militate against co-operation between prisoners even when they have found ways of coping themselves, and in any event, unique individuals will always cope in different ways. But some familiarity with the existing accounts of coping methods will help avoid making silly mistakes when talking to prisoners, and will show real concern for their position. In a few cases, it may enable the worker to make constructive suggestions drawing on the experience of others. Because 'relatives do not know how it is inside in quite the same way as Serge or Solzhenitsyn know' (Cohen & Taylor, 1972: for more on Serge, see below).

The Frustrations of Imprisonment

1. SEPARATION FROM FAMILY & FRIENDS

Prisoners are suddenly faced with learning to cope without the support of family and friends. (This presents a different set of problems for the families, considered at the end of this chapter). Research shows that prisoners with strong outside ties 'have an edge in facing pains of imprisonment' (Johnson & Toch, 1982): their knowledge that they have the support and interest of loved ones outside the prison helps them to deal with the daily frustrations of prison life and, in many cases, to maintain a hopeful attitude. This is the best outcome: unfortunately, many prisoners' relationships break down while they are in custody, and the separation from the family becomes permanent and all the more difficult to deal with. People serving long prison sentences may decide to 'freeze' their relationships with people on the outside, on the grounds that it is unfair to expect people to wait for their release, but also to avoid the pain of being rejected by the other party. Some long-termers say that this is the best way to remain friends, avoiding the bitterness of divorce. Those who try to sustain friendships and marriages often find that contacts gradually diminish.

Such problems are far worse for prisoners with young children. There is a painful dilemma as to whether or not to tell the child where the parent is, and why. Another difficult decision concerns whether to take the children to visit: many prisoners would prefer their children not to see them in prison, but a visit might help to allay children's fears. Only a minority of imprisoned mothers of young children are allowed to keep their children with them, due mainly to the shortage of places in mother and baby units in prisons, and the babies in these units lead an artificial and in many ways deprived life (White, 1989).

A recurring theme in prisoners' descriptions of the frustrations of serving a sentence is the feeling of being infantilised by the system. This operates in many different ways, including the impossibility of fulfilling family responsibilities . Someone who has been the head of a family may be unable to offer any support to the partner at times of crisis. One prisoner told me:

> when you're out there, in most cases ... you sort of keep the family together and you get the bills paid ... And when you're gone, all of a sudden, after years of not having to worry about it, they find it's not as easy as they thought it might be. And obviously it causes friction...And you're helpless in here, you can't help 'em, there's nothing you can do. And I don't think, you know, it ain't conducive with having a good, stable relationship...I mean, I'll give you a situation... but how inadequate these places can make you. I don't mean ... in your personal makeup ... Like, my father died Saturday. I can't do anything. And I feel so frustrated, so useless. There's nothing I can do to help anybody ... I should be there. That's when it hits you.

Conversely, male prisoners sometimes find that the experience of having to cope with all the problems of running a home alone, makes their wives more confident and leads them to reappraise their lives and decide to go it alone.

An unexpected finding of research into the experience of children whose fathers were imprisoned was that a significant number of male prisoners head single-parent households, and children are taken into Local Authority care as a result of their imprisonment. There were some cases where the Probation Service did not know about the children:

> Two children of a single parent father were taken into care and separated when their father was imprisoned. A mother who was unable to cope alone with her handicapped son was left alone when her husband was imprisoned for not paying a fine imposed for using a television set without a licence. Rent money in one man's possession was taken from him to offset unpaid fines but he was imprisoned for the outstanding amount, leaving his wife to try and resolve the crisis, (Shaw, 1987).

21

Women imprisoned without the opportunity to make alternative arrangements also find their children being taken into Local Authority care in large numbers.

In the case of prisoners serving long sentences, the indeterminacy of the sentence aggravates matters. Those making enquiries for the Parole Board need to be sensitive to the anger and frustration caused by uncertainty about parole prospects. Often, the prisoner feels angry on behalf of the family outside, whose hopes are also raised as parole enquiries are made:

> a lot of probation officers, they go round and lie to people's families, which is wrong. 'Cause I've seen it done a few times. One guy, who's doing a seven, was up for his first parole, I think he got a knockback, but he got told, next time he goes up, he's definitely going to get it. And this probation [officer] had been round and told his family, his kids, that he was getting it. There's no way... Then they're going round people's, like me, they go round people's houses every year, say well listen, he's up for parole, want to look at your house, blah blah blah, and it's just a lie. Because everyone knows, for a long-term prisoner, there ain't no way you're getting released within a couple of months of his E D R [earliest date of release]. So you're there every year, going to the families and building up their hopes, saying well he could get it, he could get it, if he behaves himself he could get it, and you know, whether he behaves himself or not there's no way he's getting his first parole, or second parole. (See also Hercules, 1989).

American research found that the parole process increased stress (Goodstein, 1982). This would seem to fit in with the general sense of loss of control over one's life that causes prisoners so much unease and anxiety. Great anguish is caused by rumours about the well-being and loyalty of partners outside. An indeterminate sentence makes it difficult to feel any sense of control over events in the outside world. In these circumstances, it is scarcely surprising that prisoners turn their attention to the inmate culture, and in doing so, lose their concern for what outsiders see as reality.

2. LOSS OF TOUCH AND INSTITUTIONALISATION

Prisoners describing their experiences find it hard to communicate the boring and repetitive nature of a prison sentence. In talking or writing to their families and friends, they get into the habit of putting a brave face on things, partly because honest description of the events that do temporarily give relief from the routine (such as demonstrations, fights, disciplinary measures) would cause anxiety. Discussion of the troubles of family members can increase the sense of helplessness described above, and one consequence can be that such issues are avoided, leaving very little for the prisoner and the family to discuss. Such a failure to communicate can lead to prisoners being characterised as losing touch with reality when they are in fact acutely aware of it, and of their helplessness to influence it.

A common fear among prisoners is that their minds will deteriorate. In the nature of things, their mental horizons narrow, and some prisoners become inward-looking. A prisoner wrote:

> 'What I do know is that when you first come in, you dream
> at night about what you used to do on the outside, but as
> time goes by you dream about nothing but the prison, the
> screw, the cell door, the gate, the yard. Prison is your
> whole life' (Fitzgerald, 1977).

Particularly near the beginning of a long sentence, planning for the future seems futile. Prisoners have written about the way they passed time by fantasising: for example, Trevor Hercules describes a recurrent daydream that he was one of his heroes, Bob Marley or a famous boxer (Hercules, 1989). Another prisoner spoke of conducting ferocious arguments with himself aloud in his cell:

'they sent me to see a doctor because I was doing it, ... but it's ... the way I've found of preserving my sanity.'

The tendency to withdraw can be aggravated by prescribed drugs, which are used to a disproportionate extent in women's prisons. This arose from a criminological tradition which began with writers such as Lombroso and Ferrero, who viewed women offenders as grotesque and monstrous anomalies (Bardsley, 1987). Such views were reflected in those of James Callaghan in his famous statement about the rebuilding of Holloway as a 'therapeutic' prison: 'Most women and girls in custody require some form of medical, psychiatric or remedial treatment' (House of Commons, *Hansard*, 16 December 1968).

Allen, among others, has suggested that this has enhanced the special place that 'medical personnel have historically secured for themselves in the women's prisons' (Allen, 1987).

Despite the protestations of the Home Office, it is clear that illegal drugs are also widely available in British prisons, and the system to some extent unofficially colludes with the availability of cannabis, which generally improves people's temper and makes them more docile.

Institutionalisation can take a variety of forms, which have been discussed in detail elsewhere. At one extreme, it may involve a loss of interest in the world outside prison, even to the extent that prisoners begin to fear release. The other extreme can include such a whole-hearted embrace of prison culture that prisoners turn to violence as a way of relieving pressure, accepting without question that this is the only way to survive (see, for example, Abbott, 1982, and Hercules, 1989).

Prison routine seems to take over for many people, serving if not to relieve their anxiety, at least to help them forget it. This can militate against prisoners spending much mental energy on planning for the future after release. Psychological research on adaptation to extreme situations suggests that people cope by adjusting to change so that the extreme becomes the norm, against which future changes are measured. The routine of imprisonment is accepted, which leads to the level of pain experienced by prisoners being dulled - leading in turn to a fear of institutionalisation, or of becoming a 'cabbage' (Zamble & Porporino, 1988; Cohen & Taylor, 1972).

Paradoxically, defiance of the prison regime can be a way of coping with it: 'By refusing to recognise the legitimacy of prison authority, the inmate may retain some degree of self-confidence and autonomy' (Parisi, 1982).

This is a high-risk strategy, because prisoners can become so bound up in their defiance that they serve more time: arguably the ultimate in institutionalisation. Another maladaptive reaction to stress is to attempt suicide or to mutilate oneself. The suicide rate in prisons in the U K is at least six times as high as that in the general population (Coggan & Walker, 1982). But many prisoners manage to turn their violence outwards, which may provide relief from tension although, again, at some risk.

3. FEAR - AND WORSE

Naturally enough, this culture of violence puts many prisoners in fear - including those generally regarded as being well able to look after themselves. As one prisoner said:

> you don't know who you're dealing with half the time. I mean you might call somebody a few names for whatever reason, it might be well deserved, at the time; and before you know what's happened, he's coming at you with a knife or something else. I mean, that's the situation in these places. And that's what people don't realise, you know. It doesn't matter how tough you are, you've got no answer to a knife in the back...

He went on to explain how issues of status and loss of face were involved, even where people did not want to fight. No matter how capable he might be of holding his own in a fight, he feared for his life (and this in a relatively relaxed prison regime). The American murderer, Jack Henry Abbott, confirmed this from his own experience: 'Most prisoners fear almost every other prisoner around them' (Abbott, 1982) and Hercules makes the same point (Hercules, 1989).

If men like these live in fear, how much more so do those convicted (or rumoured to be) of sexual offences against children.

Such prisoners serving their sentences on normal location sometimes find the nature of the offence coming to light,

> and can be attacked with any weapon to hand, by prisoners, sometimes in collusion with staff. They are followed by a wall of silence, due to the inmate code about informing (Coggan & Walker, 1982).

This also creates the necessary climate for such activities as baroning and manipulation of other prisoners into giving up their precious cigarettes or money. Similarly, sexual victimisation can be concealed, and can 'force some individuals over the brink into serious difficulty' (Bowker, 1982).

Apart from fear, prison breeds a lack of trust in others. Information entrusted to other prisoners might be used against one, so in practice prisoners seem rarely to confide in each other. Oddly, because all are subject to similar stresses, this tends to be given as a reason not to share their feelings: prisoners say that they do not discuss their depression with others because this would remind them of their own predicament. Possibly because of the macho culture of male prisons, this seems to be the norm, rather than any tendency to share information about coping mechanisms. Intimate contact is avoided, socialising being kept on a superficial level. Some observers have suggested that this serves a number of purposes. It makes people feel safer, and it helps to preserve individuals' autonomy and freedom of action, if only by making it easier to avoid being drawn into other people's fights (Zamble & Porporino, 1988).

It is hard to generalise reliably, but there is some evidence that women deal with these matters rather differently. Recent accounts by ex-prisoners include details of women protecting vulnerable inmates (Carlen et al, 1985, pp.175-6; Padel & Stevenson, 1988, p.105) and giving advice, friendship and warmth to others (Carlen et al, 1985, pp.131-2, 155; Padel & Stevenson, 1988, pp.102, 131; Bardsley, 1987, pp.71, 94-5; Franey, 1989). It may be that women are less reluctant to describe such episodes, or that they are more common in women's prisons.

The atmosphere of fear can tip over into outright paranoia, at least for short periods in individuals' prison careers. People become less trusting, and withdraw from involvement with others. This can spill over into their relationships with people outside. As one prisoner said, 'it's very hard...to trust people, to totally trust them. I mean, specially anybody in authority... I mean, you do get paranoid. When you're locked up on your own a lot, like'.

For some people, this leads to withdrawal from any contact with others, to the extent that they prefer the conditions in the punishment block to their normal location. In some prisons, particularly those specialising with long-term prisoners, segregation is made available as a matter of choice, so that prisoners do not have to break the rules in order to be segregated. Again, Hercules confirms this:

> As time wore on in Albany, I found myself getting into more and more trouble, and to be quite honest sometimes I welcomed the block to get away from the tension of the hate-filled wing with its overpowering sense of hopelessness. Whether prisoners admit it to themselves or not, most of them become paranoid at times' (Hercules, 1989).

He goes on to say that he preferred to be in the block because 'I didn't fancy being regimented like some cabbage with the rest of them'.

In some prisons, extreme security arrangements can worsen the atmosphere and provide a justification for feelings of persecution and being watched. Carole Richardson described in an interview her feelings on first going into Durham 'H' Wing: 'views of nothing ... cameras on you 24 hours a day ... being watched; knowing that whatever you wanted to do someone would see you. If you wanted to cry, they'd watch you cry' (Franey, 1989).

This problem is made worse for women prisoners because so few of them merit conditions of maximum security that such placements are used as a punishment for less serious offenders who make life difficult for staff in other prisons.

As many as one quarter of those interviewed for a study at Grendon Underwood psychiatric prison in England were 'pathologically depressed' (Gunn et al, 1978; see also Zamble & Porporino, 1988).

A general atmosphere of bitterness has been noted by many observers. A prison governor with 25 years' service said:

I think you'll find more bitterness and self-pity in prisons than in any other place on earth, because prisons are the nearest things to hells-on-earth that have ever been created. To people who can't stand bitterness or think there is something distasteful about self-pity, all I'd say is, "Well stop and ask yourself if you're sure you're such a fine character that you wouldn't be like that yourself if you were inside?" If their answer was that they're sure they wouldn't, I'd think they'd very little imagination and no self-knowledge (Parker, 1973).

Specific Deprivations of Prisoners

Conceptually, it makes little sense to search for the psychological effects of imprisonment without acknowledging that these effects may vary considerably across individuals (Zamble & Porporino, 1988).

It seems likely that this error, of introducing spurious 'scientific' methods into the study of reactions to imprisonment, has contributed a good deal to the rather sterile debate about whether or not long-term prisoners deteriorate whilst in prison. Some of them argue that the reverse has been true for them, but there can be little doubt that most people serving long prison sentences change during, and perhaps due to, their imprisonment.

What follows is not intended to deny the individuality of responses to imprisonment, but rather to draw attention to some common experiences.

1. SEXUAL

Clearly, people's sexual lives change when they are imprisoned. Their sexual feelings do not seem to change much, but there is very limited scope for the expression of heterosexual feelings, and the practice of homosexuality is illegal for male prisoners (on the grounds that a prison is not a 'private place' within the terms of the Sexual Offences Act). This has a number of implications. First, sexuality is thwarted or forced underground. Second, no help is offered with protection from sexually-transmitted diseases (and the refusal to provide condoms to prisoners continues to be justified by the Home Office in terms of the need to avoid condoning illegal behaviour). Thirdly, men's sexuality becomes a form of currency, with apparently weak prisoners victimised sexually.

The introduction of conjugal visits in prison systems overseas has been quite encouraging, but the climate will have to change considerably in this country before this can happen. A proposed experiment some years ago involving visits by women prisoners' children and their carers, using Portakabins, was thwarted on security grounds - but also, according to some observers, because prison officers objected to the idea as 'the thin end of the wedge', leading towards the introduction of conjugal visits. An experiment is, however, under way at Holloway prison, and the Woolf Report made far-reaching recommendations on home leave and family visits (Woolf, 1991).

2. LOSS OF PRIVACY

Obviously, prisoners suffer from the loss of personal privacy. It is hard for outsiders to imagine how extreme this is, and easy to be surprised when long-term prisoners express a preference for being locked alone in their cells rather than 'allowed' association with other prisoners. To understand this, one has to recall some of the facts of imprisonment in this country.

Remand prisoners are likely to be housed two or three to a cell. In most remand prisons, this involves sharing a very small cell and, in the absence of integral sanitation, using a chamber pot at night in the presence of others. Prisoners have described serious digestive complaints resulting from constantly refusing to suffer this indignity and forcing themselves to wait until the morning. In the older prisons, toilet facilities and showers are communal, in the 'recesses' on the wings, and the toilets have cut-away doors.

Cells are regularly searched without notice, and prisoners are moved with very little warning. Personal effects are sometimes broken during searches, and do not always find their way to the new prison with the owner. If they do, there can be long delays.

Letters are censored (though only a sample is now read in lower-security prisons) and visits are supervised. In many modern prisons, video surveillance supplements the watchful eyes of uniformed and other staff. In most prisons, there is little time when inmates can move around unescorted.

Details of prisoners' offences and such things as the trial depositions of witnesses are available to staff, as are the 'confidential' social reports . Sensitive medical information may also become common knowledge, including for example the results of HIV tests. In prisons where uniformed staff are involved in welfare or personal officer schemes, wing staff are encouraged to read prisoners' files (to which the prisoners themselves have no access).

Not surprisingly, prisoners begin to feel that staff seem to know more about them than they know themselves. Any time in private is cherished. But even alone in their cells, they can be examined through peep-holes, and the lights are normally controlled from outside the cell.

3. LOSS OF INDEPENDENCE

Toch has drawn attention to the ways in which prisoners respond when some of their capability for independent action is restored to them. In therapeutic prison regimes, and in ordinary prisons where an attempt is made to treat prisoners more as normal people, some of the destructive norms of prison life can be broken down. Where staff consciously work to improve prisoners' self-esteem, and respect their individuality, relations between them and inmates not surprisingly improve. Where it is recognised that prisoners are worthwhile individuals who want to make a contribution to society, they respond. Toch gives the rather limited examples of charitable fundraising, drug trials and competitions involving art and literature (but note that drug trials on prisoners are illegal in the U.K.). Creativity is stifled in prison if conscious efforts are not made to avoid this (Johnson & Toch, 1982).

Another way is to provide educational facilities - and in many ways, the prison education service has an admirable record. But its successes are mainly in the training and long-term prisons: educational facilities are much sparser in other prisons.

'Education is a constant source of tension and conflict between the poorly educated screws and the more articulate prisoners. Inmates who have achieved any sort of academic qualifications often feel that they do so despite, and not because of, the prison staff and facilities. In many ways, education in prison appears to be designed to prevent the prisoner from acquiring an understanding of himself and his situation. Inside the front cover of every prison exercise book, for example, you will read that you are not permitted to write about yourself, prison conditions, your offences, sentences, other inmates' lives, or methods of committing crime. You must not depict the prison staff, prison conditions, or other prisoners. Naturally enough, you must not write, paint or draw anything obscene or against the security, good order and discipline of the prison. Imagine for a moment that you have served a year inside, spending twenty-three out of twenty-four hours every day, every week, in your cell. What could you produce in that exercise book which did not contravene the rules? ' (Fitzgerald, 1977).

Educational facilities in British prisons are always subordinated to the requirements of security, and this can be abused. For example, a prisoner who is about to sit an examination may be moved to another prison where it is impossible to do so, or a prisoner completing a correspondence course may be moved to a prison where there are restrictions on the number of books each inmate may have, or on the amount of mail received. Such transfers happen fairly often, and can be used as an informal disciplinary measure.

Independence is further compromised by many other petty rules, and by a lack of any say over 'allocation': prisoners are moved when suspected of trouble-making, without any investigation or notice, and families sometimes travel long distances only to find that a prisoner has recently been moved or is in transit.

'In the case of a prisoner's cell, familiarity doesn't breed contempt. On the contrary, a prisoner begins to feel that this is his 'home', the centre of his world. A well-known technique of secret police to 'break' a prisoner is to move him from his own cell to a strange one, in another prison, quite arbitrarily, in the middle of the night, and without warning. This procedure, 'ghosting', is accepted and common practice in British prisons ' (Fitzgerald, 1977).

The Home Office Circular permitting this practice has come to be used as an alternative, and unaccountable, disciplinary measure, not subject to outside review, and has been criticised on civil liberties grounds (Gostin & Staunton, 1985).

It is hard to avoid concluding, as Jimmy Boyle does in his smuggled prison diary, that prison is doing the opposite of what it should, when it limits and diminishes the individual's sense of responsibility.

4. LOSS OF STRUCTURE

It may seem paradoxical to suggest that prisoners, forced into an almost totally structured environment, suffer from a loss of structure. But there is a good deal of evidence for this. Time becomes very difficult to manage when one's control over its use has been removed. Many prison writings testify to this. 'The problem of time is everything. Nothing distinguishes one hour from the next' as Victor Serge put it;

> The value of an hour changes, and all the apparatus built up over the years for dealing with the passage of time suddenly becomes obsolete. In normal life, few hours are entirely without incident or interest. In prison, many hours might pass, in which nothing happens. It becomes possible to look at a clock without receiving any information from it. It is not that time becomes irrelevant. In many senses, it becomes more important, for in the end, that is what it's all about. No. It is merely that measured as the outside world measures it, time becomes intolerable. The prisoner has to learn how to deal with the passage of time in a different way. (Serge, 1970).

A good deal more has been written about this phenomenon, both in prison autobiographies and, in a more theoretical vein, by Cohen and Taylor in *Psychological Survival* (1977) and by Farber (1944). Suffice it to say that the management of time is a problem all prisoners have to deal with, and some never find a satisfactory way of doing so.

5. LOSS OF RIGHTS

It may seem to be stating the obvious to say that prisoners suffer from a loss of civil rights, but it is worth reflecting upon the extent to which this is true.

The legal position is that they continue to have any of the rights of the citizen which have not been specifically removed from them by virtue of their imprisonment - for example, they have no right to vote or to stand for office, but they retain the right of access to the courts. In practice, many of the rights people outside take for granted are denied to prisoners, and even basic things like the right to legal advice and representation are hedged about with restrictions - some of which have been removed in recent years as a result of European court decisions: as Treverton-Jones puts it: 'the courts have come increasingly to regard unimpeded access to legal advice and assistance as an integral part of unimpeded access to the courts' (Treverton-Jones, 1989).

Prison discipline is thus increasingly subject to legal regulation, and since the 1976 Hull riot, courts are more willing to review decisions of disciplinary hearings. Litigation by prisoners has accordingly increased, and Boards of Visitors now have discretion to allow prisoners to be legally represented for disciplinary hearings.

The Prior Committee, which reported in 1985, and subsequent recommendations by the Chief Inspector of Prisons, have led to some of the old Prison Rules being abolished, so that for example there is no longer an offence of making malicious allegations against prison officers. Nevertheless, the Chief Inspector's reports continue to give examples which show that disciplinary hearings fail to ensure that prisoners are dealt with according to basic standards of justice, uniformed staff even being allowed to adopt menacing postures towards accused prisoners during hearings, and the disciplinary system is in need of radical reform (Scraton et al, 1991; Woolf Report, 1991).

Some of the bodies charged with protecting the rights of prisoners have persistently been accused of toothlessness. Boards of Visitors, for example, are mainly composed of respectable establishment figures, often busy people, whose approach tends to be reactive, effectively allowing the professional prison staff to set the agenda. Although members of the Boards are required to make regular but unpredictable visits to prisons, most of them give some notice and when particular courses of action are felt to require a Board member as a witness, governors have some discretion as to which Board member they invite (Vagg, 1985, and personal observation). The Ombudsman has some, limited responsibilities in respect of prisons, but has been largely ineffective in carrying them out (Birkinshaw, 1985). Overall, compared to other countries, Britain has a poor record where the accountability of prisons for the treatment of their inmates is concerned, and the number of cases going to the European courts reflects this.

The effect of this is often a feeling of powerlessness on the part of individual prisoners: the system seems unassailable. Lack of accountability is aggravated by the secrecy with which much of the British prison system operates (although this has lessened). When anything untoward is happening in a prison, civilian staff can be excluded. During the 1979 disturbances at Wormwood Scrubs, probation officers were unaware of what was happening - and when a prison visitor and a probation volunteer exposed some of what had occurred, their appointments were terminated. This could easily happen again. There has, however, been considerable progress: the obsessive secrecy described by Cohen and Taylor in *Prison Secrets* no longer prevails.

Prisoners who have been recommended for deportation have a particular problem in this respect. Deportees can be removed from the country at very short notice, with no time to sort out their affairs, and those who are reluctant to leave are sometimes drugged and put into strait-jackets to effect their removal. There is no automatic system for referral of deportation prisoners to the probation welfare service, who may not even be aware of their existence. There is a scheme in the Midlands run by the Joint Council for the Welfare of Immigrants, under which the prison probation department refers prisoners for expert assistance, but this does not cover other parts of the country. Deportees are disadvantaged when it comes to parole, and are increasingly likely to be held in the largely unaccountable private remand system (D'Orey, 1984; see also Chapter Five).

6. LOSS OF 'SELF'

The fear many prisoners have is that the experience of prison will change them in ways they cannot control. The fear of deterioration relates not only to physical health (and in fact many male prisoners work on their physique and leave prison fitter and stronger) but more to mental health. There is a concern about becoming institutionalised, and a fear of becoming a 'cabbage'. This is documented very fully by Cohen and Taylor in *Psychological Survival* , and is mentioned repeatedly in the autobiographical literature.

There is also a more general fear of becoming excessively hardened, best described in Abbott's words: 'So we can all hold up like good soldiers and harden ourselves in prison. But if you do that for too long, you lose yourself' (Abbott, 1982).

The other deprivations mentioned above make it difficult to trust others, and a prolonged period of not opening oneself up to others can damage the ability to do so. This makes contacts with the outside all the more important.

To some extent, prison regimes are deliberately designed to damage prisoners' sense of self. Prisons, as large bureaucratic organisations, need to find ways of processing individuals. To do so, standardised routines are imposed. But the process goes further, in that total institutions are based upon the assumption that everything will run better if individuals' uniqueness is played down. Officers and inmates are therefore forced into uniformity. New arrivals are systematically stripped of their symbols of personal identity: names are replaced by numbers; clothes by prison uniform; personal possessions are taken away, to be symbolically returned upon release. The process is described and analysed in sociological terms in Goffman's *Asylums*, and examples of how it feels to individual prisoners are quoted in Priestley (1989).

This process is the beginning of the institutionalisation that makes release seem so threatening for many prisoners (see Chapter Four). In many prisons, it is made worse by the removal of individuals' autonomy in making important decisions: the demands of the prison as a bureaucracy mean that prisoners cannot decide for themselves about whether they need medical attention or whether to enrol for an educational course. But the system is set up to take this loss of independence a step further, so that a member of the uniformed staff acts as a gate-keeper, screening requests for access to a doctor or a probation officer, or applications for legal aid. Sometimes it is impossible even to obtain basic necessities like sanitary towels without a demeaning request to a prison officer, and the quest for luxuries like a birthday card for a family member needs planning weeks in advance.

COPING STRATEGIES

There is a danger of concentrating solely upon negative aspects of imprisonment. What heartens many people who work with prisoners is their resilience and dignity in the face of pain and indignities. Sometimes conscious strategies are adopted to deal with a sentence, and to an outsider some of these seem futile or self-deluding. But we must not presume we know better than a prisoner how he or she should do their time, and it is a very brave or stupid outsider who criticises prisoners for their coping strategies. Some sociological accounts have come close to doing so, and few prisoners fit neatly into their sometimes rather glib typologies of coping. The trouble with the positivistic research reports about this issue is that they tend to fail to respond to human uniqueness and 'at worst, define it away' (Johnson & Toch, 1982): differences between individuals are treated as sampling errors rather than as data in themselves.

Some of the writers about inmate behaviour in concentration camps such as Bettelheim and Heimler have shown how survival was aided by mental resources developed in earlier life:

> autonomy, self-respect, inner integration, a rich inner life, and the ability to relate to others in meaningful ways were the psychological conditions which, more than any others, permitted one to survive in the camps as much a whole human being as conditions and chance would permit (Bettelheim, 1979).

Transferring this analysis to ordinary prisoners of course begs a lot of questions, and Cohen & Taylor admit that they over-stated this (Cohen & Taylor, 1976). What is interesting is that some prisoners seem to find such inner resources. Bettelheim's list emphasises qualities valued by educated, middle-class people, and yet the predominantly working-class population of prisons often come to value similar qualities and to base their survival strategies upon them. Perhaps there is something in Abbott's defiantly romantic view of prisoners:

> There is a paradox at the core of penology, and from it derive the thousand ills and afflictions of the prison system. It is that not only the worst of the young are sent to prison, but the best - that is, the proudest, the bravest, the most daring, the most enterprising, and the most undefeated of the poor (Abbott, 1982).

Certainly, long-term prisoners have more opportunities to devise coping strategies, partly because of the different regimes in which they serve out their time. It may be that necessity is the mother of invention, and that this explains the variety of strategies adopted. People respond to difficulties in varying ways because they are unique individuals but we can observe some patterns. It is worth remembering, however, that seemingly contradictory coping mechanisms may be of use to prisoners - and may therefore be employed - in different circumstances and at various stages of a sentence.

1. DEFIANCE

For some prisoners, the system which confines them is so outrageously unjust that they can maintain their dignity only by defying it - although to varying degrees, as total opposition to the system is counter-productive, since it need never compromise. Defiance may also be destructive in another sense: people can lose themselves altogether in their battles against an all-powerful system, and become consumed by hate (which will remove any possibility of parole). But the prisoner who resists 'has a chance to avoid disintegration of his personality so long as he will go on resisting the moral pressure, and accept hardships which result from being a 'recalcitrant prisoner'' (Hermann, 1974).

While such resistance is dangerous, it has important benefits in terms of dignity, and for some, hate is functional, 'because people often need to hate to be able to resist' (Hermann, 1974). Similar points are made by prisoners in Britain. James Campbell interviewed a man who had carried out a seemingly futile roof-top protest. Discussing his motivation, it became clear that it 'was crucial to his continuing sense of himself, it was his way of confirming that he had, after all, some worth in this wilderness, of making his voice heard and defeating the insufferable torment of remaining silent. Pointless it may have been, but it was none the less a necessary act' (Campbell, 1986).

There is a sense in which prisoners assert, by their defiance, that they do not accept the norms the prison is trying to impose and the person who can 'adjust' to prison may never be able to adjust to life outside again (see for example Abbott, 1982, p.14). Personality theorists have shown that the enhancement of one's self esteem is a basic human need, and a system that attacks self-esteem in so many ways is bound to have to deal with some who feel that this need is worth taking considerable risks to assert. Cohen & Taylor describe prisoners' sense of satisfaction in moving from powerlessness in the face of a strict regime, through continuous struggle to achieve 'gradual increments of autonomy' (Cohen & Taylor, 1972). Similarly, Jimmy Boyle catalogues the struggle over a number of years to make a success of the Barlinnie Special Unit and to defend the gains represented for prisoners by its establishment, and a study of the Peterhead riot shows how it arose partly from protests against a violent and uncompromising regime (Scraton et al, 1991).

In American prisons, and to some extent in recent years in the U.K., this defiance has taken the form of racial solidarity. For some prisoners, it becomes a point of pride to question everything about the system, which represents for them the violence of the whole society against black communities. Jack Henry Abbott has written vividly about this:

> It is a maxim that the morally strongest and the most intelligent among an oppressed people are to be found on the scaffolds and in the prisons of the oppressors. I have spent a lifetime in prisons with American Indians, Mexicans and Chicanos, and black Americans. Without ques-

> tion every non-white prisoner I have known is grappling
> with a revolutionary consciousness of the world - but the
> most consistent, the most persistent, are black prisoners
> (Abbott, 1982).

This formulates the unstated fear of prison administrators in this country, that black prisoners will become organised. Uniformed prison staff seem to feel that race relations is no problem in British prisons, at the same time holding beliefs which exacerbate such problems: they view black prisoners as arrogant, hostile to authority and to law and order, belligerent, demanding, noisy, lazy, unintelligent and having chips on their shoulders (Genders & Players, 1989). Most black prisoners seem not to regard such prejudices as causing them major problems at present, but this could change rapidly, while prison officers' occupational culture is unlikely to be altered by present Home Office policies, liberal as they are. As both the CRE and the Society of Black Lawyers have pointed out, while the Home Office race relations policy is exemplary on paper, it is not so impressive in practice (Prison Reform Trust, 1989). Despite recent changes in the Prison Rules, inmates fear intimidation if they complain to Race Relations Liaison Officers, if they know of their existence (Carvel, 1990).

2. CAMPAIGNING

A closely allied strategy to defiance is campaigning. Some prisoners use the rhetoric and rules of the prison system to undermine it or to improve their own position. The barrack-room lawyer in prison is a figure in popular mythology, and does exist. One criminologist has suggested that 'censoriousness' by prisoners, attempting to hold prison staff to the rules, implies acceptance of the system. This is debatable (and in any case, many prisoners are deeply conservative individuals!). For some inmates, there is a bitter satisfaction in exposing contradictions, showing up injustice. As he goes on to say, this 'seems to mitigate many of the pains of imprisonment' (Mathiesen, 1965), which seems sufficient justification (see also Cohen & Taylor, 1972). Such activities can help to build up solidarity between inmates, who then support each other more as individuals.

The increased possibility of access to the courts has certainly led to more of this kind of activity, as its success became apparent. Litigation by prisoners has had a considerable impact upon Home Office policy in recent years, and many of the recent reforms in prison secrecy and censorship have been achieved in this way, particularly when backed by organisations such as the National Council for Civil Liberties, taking cases to the European courts.

There is also a long tradition in the U.K. of ex-prisoners becoming involved in campaigning about the prison system, which is arguably a rare example of people learning skills in prison which stand them in good stead upon release. Ever since the pacifists and suffrage campaigners at the beginning of the century, middle-class ex-prisoners have campaigned about penal reform. More recently, ex-prisoners have become involved in welfare projects for serving prisoners and those who need help on their release, including imaginative projects combining campaigning and welfare work such as the Creative and Supportive Trust in London, which is associated with housing projects, a theatre group, advice work and a number of other activities. Other ex-prisoners' groups have mainly concentrated upon campaigning and information work, such as Women in Prison and PROP (see appendix for further information).

3. CARE FOR OTHERS

There is also, of course, considerable scope for individuals in prison to care for each other - and in some circumstances, for people in need outside.

Campbell noted that although the boredom of prisoners was his overriding impression, little things stood out despite the austere atmosphere. He found that the austerity created 'not only the paranoia which threatens life, but also the sensitivity - one of the most impressive sights in the prison - which insists on celebrating it' (Campbell, 1986).

Both Cohen & Taylor's study and Boyle's autobiographical account show many examples of prisoners getting together to protect themselves or vulnerable individuals - but such material is relatively uncommon, perhaps because it violates the male inmate code, the norm that says that everyone has to do his own time.

It is also well known that, despite very low wages, prisoners frequently raise substantial sums of money for charity. This is often presented in the press as paradoxical, but if people are complex and rounded, can offenders not express and act upon a wish to make amends? Prison chaplains, who are generally far from being naive, say that one of the pleasures of their work is the scope for creating opportunities for people to change themselves.

4. ALLIANCES WITH PRISON STAFF

Many prisoners want as little as possible to do with the uniformed staff. That said, many others are prepared to make alliances with their custodians, and some form friendly relationships. A prison designed to rehabilitate prisoners would have to depend to a large extent upon human relationships, and prisoners are judged as to their suitability for early release on parole partly by their expressed attitudes to staff. The area is therefore a complex one to examine, because people do not necessarily express their true feelings.

Not all prison officers welcome or accept cordiality between themselves and prisoners: in some ways, perhaps, the job is simpler without such complications. But it has been suggested that Goffman's description of 'people workers' applies to prison officers, and many of their transactions with prisoners are personal in nature. This includes negotiating compliance with the rules. The complications arise where this approach conflicts with a bureaucratic one: the application of standardised rules in an impartial way is also part of the job. Nevertheless, prison officers frequently become involved in advice-giving and counselling with prisoners, particularly those they know well. The evidence is that they tend to regard this as over and above their normal job, and to see it as 'real' help, contrasting it with the help given by civilian staff whose paid work it is (Lombardo, 1981).

Cohen & Taylor noted that prisoners protected not only themselves but also the staff from violent inmates (1972). The class background of many staff is very similar to that of prisoners, and in some ways they have a lot in common. Prisoners regarded as 'respectable' seem to do well in areas where favourable treatment is at the discretion of officers. In some cases, prisoners come from the same home town as prison officers and they discuss this as a pastime and, for the prisoner, as a way of keeping up-to-date with the kind of changes their visitors would be unlikely to discuss (for example, physical alterations to a town).

As one life-sentence prisoner put it: 'I'll talk about any topic that I want to if I'm talking to a member of the uniformed staff. It shows that I've seen something there that goes beyond the uniform.'

5. 'SELF-IMPROVEMENT'

For some prisoners, the sentence is treated as an opportunity. This takes a variety of forms, but remarkable things have been achieved by prisoners in recent years, considering the constraints of prison life.

The Home Office refers to a 'career' for prisoners serving life sentences. Although official recognition of this concept occurred only in the 1980s, it has been understood by prisoners, at least intuitively, for much longer. Some prisoners consciously follow an educational career, from GCSEs to postgraduate work (though this is only possible with the facilities provided for those serving very long sentences). Others work on their bodies, building themselves up to championship standards in weightlifting or other sports. Such activities represent a use of time that can be seen to have resulted in personal achievement. Others make it a point of pride to gain a thorough understanding of the institution of imprisonment and its effects upon them - a version of the survival strategy found in the autobiographies of many survivors of concentration camps in the last war (Cohen & Taylor, 1972; Bettelheim, 1979).

Prisoners may pursue trade training, not with any optimism about obtaining work upon release (some of the trades offered being almost obsolete, and many of the prisoners having no history of employment). Work is seen as a strategy for passing time, and prison work is highly valued: 'In prison it is a fundamental rule of mental hygiene to work at all costs, to occupy the mind' (Serge, 1970).

There is also, for a minority, an interest in self- development at a deeper level, by the pursuit of religious or philosophical ideas:

> Among those who succeed in resisting madness, their
> intense inner life brings them to a higher conception of
> life, to a deeper consciousness of the self, its value, its
> strength. A victory over jail is a great victory. At certain
> moments you feel astonishingly free . You sense that if
> this torture has not broken you, nothing will ever be able
> to break you (Serge, 1970).

Thus, as one modern prisoner put it, 'A dispersal prison provides
the degree of freedom necessary to exercise personal choice.'

There is, of course, also a substantial literature of prisoners'
conversions to Christianity.

Conventional academic studies offer some prisoners a route to
self-esteem and self-fulfilment, and a constructive way of passing
the time. Prisoners sometimes study at night when the prison is
quiet, and find that this makes up for what they regard as a lack of
stimulation in the normal prison environment.

6. DRUGS

Relatively simple to obtain in most prisons, drugs offer an easier
means of escape. According to some prisoners, it is only cannabis
that 'keeps the lid on the place' (Campbell, 1986). Information on
this area is of course very hard for outsiders to obtain , but there is
also evidence of the use of drugs by injection in many U.K. prisons,
with consequent concern about the spread of disease (Prison Reform
Trust, 1988). Drug use in prisons causes problems for individuals,
even if it presents no particular control problems to the system.
Prisoners who get into debt may be in danger from others, and elect
to go into segregated conditions. Sometimes, pressure is put on
their families outside to pay such debts. Such pressures can also
lead to prisoners being pressured into smuggling drugs on their
return from home leave.

7. CONTACTS WITH THE OUTSIDE WORLD

The welfare professionals working with prisoners from the
outside are relatively powerless, and it is easy for the prison

authorities to exclude or marginalise troublesome outsiders. However, the involvement of outside individuals and groups remains important to prisoners, and for people in total institutions generally, the knowledge that there are people outside who love and care about them helps maintain their identity and sanity, their will to go on.

The Effects of Imprisonment upon Prisoners' Spouses and Children

Clearly, a partner of a prisoner will face many of the problems common to couples separated by things outside their control, as will prisoners' children. There are, however, additional factors where prisoners' families are concerned: it is not enough to treat them as typical single-parent families (Matthews, 1983).

Something like 10,000 children every year suffer the problems associated with their father going to prison, and a significant number of mothers are also imprisoned. Although these problems have not often been studied, they are real and painful. Indeed, one researcher has suggested that they often exceed the suffering of victims of offences (Shaw, 1981). A volunteer working with prisoners' families observed that 'the children of prisoners suffer greatly, partly because of the difficulties of adjusting to living without someone whom they know exists' (quoted in Matthews, 1983).

The prisoner is removed for reasons which young children cannot understand. For older children, there is a stigma attached to imprisonment. On the one hand, they are proud of their parent; on the other, they are bullied by other children who pass on their own parents' views about the offender. There can be considerable guilt and confusion about the reasons for the parent's removal.

For the spouse left at home, there are great difficulties, many of which no longer face the imprisoned partner: budgeting, childcare, accommodation problems, loneliness, fears about readjustment after the prisoner's release, sexual harassment, stigmatisation in their home areas, the problems of visiting a distant prison and so on. Shaw reported that 'Many times during the course of the research [...] wives of prisoners explained with bitterness that they and their children - not their husbands - were 'serving the sentence' (Shaw, 1981).

When, reversing the normal practice of going by the wishes of the prisoner, the Probation Service in Nottinghamshire asked families whether they would welcome contact from a probation volunteer, the take-up increased to an unprecedented 95%. Areas of work undertaken included support through the immediate crisis of the partner's imprisonment, advice on dealing with children's reactions, marital counselling and information about the prison and benefits systems (Monger et al, 1981):

> The children of imprisoned mothers may not show physical signs but there is no doubt of the misery and suffering they feel. They suffer isolation and rejection at school, show behaviour problems and experience difficulties with school work. There is often regression in developmental skills, hyperactivity (which makes visiting more difficult) and psychological withdrawal (White, 1989).

This suggests that probation officers should give a higher priority than they often do to maintaining contact with prisoners' families. Two large studies confirm this: according to Pauline Morris, 'Almost all those interviewed felt that someone should visit them when their husband was convicted to see if they were all right' (Morris, 1964).

Monger and his colleagues concluded that 'monthly contacts - as long as regular and predictable - could be the vehicle of much useful help. Most if not all probation officers could afford to carry and work with at least a handful of throughcare cases on that basis' (Monger et al, 1981).

The involvement of other professionals can be important, too. Contact with a social worker, probation officer or health visitor can open the way for families unfamiliar with the range of services available to a whole network of other possibly helpful agencies.

An immediate difficulty faced by the partner of a prisoner with children is what to tell them about his or her disappearance. Studies of adoption have shown how harmful it is for children to be subjected to sudden, unplanned disclosure of unpalatable information - but when a parent's imprisonment is concealed, there is always a danger that it will be revealed in malicious gossip. A particularly invidious situation is created if the older children know the truth but are expected to keep it hidden from the younger ones. The danger is that the parents' needs may be put before those of the children. Matters are doubtless made worse by popular beliefs about sentencing policy: most people are unaware of the relatively trivial offences for which people are imprisoned, which is bound to increase the stigma attached to imprisonment. On balance, it seems better to advise people to be honest with children wherever possible, both about what the prisoner did and where he or she is. This opens the subject up for discussion and reduces the likelihood of harmful fantasising (Shaw, 1981).

Sometimes, partners are made to feel that they were in some way responsible for the offence. Particularly in close communities, even children of offenders may be threatened or attacked (Barry, 1989). Where offences have been committed against the prisoner's children or stepchildren, there is a tendency, even among some workers in caring services, to assume that the children's mother colluded with the offending and to blame her.

Financial difficulties often follow the imprisonment of a partner. This is more likely to apply where the prisoner has been the main earner, but also arises with couples and families on benefits. The Department of Social Security finances only one visit every few weeks (although the recommendations of the Woolf Report led to an improvement) but many prisons allow more frequent visits and prisoners not unnaturally encourage their families to come as often as possible. Similarly, family finances can suffer when someone is imprisoned for fine default, where there is pressure to raise the money to 'buy out' the prisoner. Sometimes, debts come to light which the prisoner has no means of paying, but not all partners have the skills or knowledge to deal with creditors - although large institutions such as local authorities and fuel boards can often be persuaded to delay enforcement measures. Some families continue to try to pay fines for previous offences, not knowing that these can be 'lodged' by the sentencing court (that is, written off in recognition of prisoners' inability to pay).

We have already seen that the prisoner's world tends to shrink during the sentence. This is often taken as evidence of selfishness. Certainly, prisoners frequently perceive their own immediate deprivations and problems more acutely than those of their families. When both parties were asked to rate the gravity of their problems, 'the problems voiced by the man in prison did not match those expressed by his wife. In many cases inmates made no mention of their children as a specific factor causing concern' (Shaw, 1981).

In fact, prisoners' spouses tend to keep problems from them, to avoid increasing their worries, just as prisoners conceal their own anxieties from their families on the grounds that disclosure will not make things any easier. Nevertheless, a distinct pattern emerges, of male prisoners giving 'self-centred replies' while women partners said that the prisoner was 'alright inside' compared to the problems the women had to face outside (Shaw, 1981). This, combined with a shrinking perspective on the prisoner's part and the communication problems already discussed, can drive couples apart no matter how hard each partner tries to understand the position of the other. Many male offenders are imprisoned repeatedly, and partners lose patience with their inability to avoid imprisonment and their apparent indifference to it.

There are cases where a break in the relationship between prisoner and partner can be a good thing. Many partnerships founder because the prisoner, on the one hand, becomes more dependent upon the partner while the person outside is forced by circumstances to develop independence.

Where relationships are already troubled, imprisonment can provide the opportunity for the free partner to end them, or to receive advice from others that was not previously available. Thus, some children are better off when their father is imprisoned. Even they, however, need support in dealing with what has happened (Shaw, 1981), although no substantial resources have so far been provided for work of this kind. Not surprisingly, women who have to cope alone for the first time in a relationship become more assertive and independent. Sometimes this is encouraged by involvement in 'wives' groups' run by the Probation Service and by making childcare arrangements co-operatively. One of the most difficult adjustments for prisoners whose relationship survives their sentence is to accept the growth and change that may have occurred in the partner as a result of the sentence.

Penal reformers' suggestions on how to alleviate some of these problems have largely fallen on stony ground. The Radzinowicz

Committee recommended experimenting with conjugal visits for long-term prisoners as long ago as 1968,. Although such a system is common in other countries, it has been resisted on security grounds by prison officers in this country. The Chair of the Styal branch of the Prison Officers' Association told a House of Commons Committee in 1978, when asked about a proposed experiment under which adult visitors would escort female prisoners' children to stay with them in the grounds of the prison, 'The staff will not allow them through the gate. They are unanimous; they are all standing together. It is not just the staff at Styal prison' (quoted in Matthews, 1983).

At the time, security was given as the reason. More recently, the Association has suggested that another point at issue was the possible 'breakdown of relationships with the surrounding civil community' (Bartell, 1989).

Similarly, Britain compares unfavourably with other countries in terms of home leave provision for prisoners, although it is becoming increasingly common towards the end of longer sentences, and the Woolf Report encouraged policy changes (Woolf, 1991).

There is now a wide range of voluntary organisations offering help to prisoners' families on a local basis: details of how to contact them are given in the Appendix.

3. Who Works with Prisoners?

A wide variety of people have a range of responsibilities for prisoners, and this chapter describes the work of the main groups of workers responsible for prisoners' welfare. With so many different people involved, prisoners can get confused about who does what: the scope for liaison between the different workers is therefore examined. Finally, some of the limitations the prison places upon professional workers are considered, including the difficulties likely to be faced by women and black workers confronting the 'culture' of male prisons.

FIELD PROBATION OFFICERS

The Probation Service in many areas arranges matters so that all prisoners are allocated a probation officer outside. This has come to be known as 'throughcare'. Unfortunately, the provision of this service in practice is patchy, and some Probation Services explicitly say that it should be given a low priority. This has been particularly the case since the Home Office published its *Statement of National Objectives and Priorities* in 1984 .

In what follows, the best practice will be described, since it is on offer, at least in theory, to prisoners from the majority of areas in England, Wales and Northern Ireland. In Scotland, the situation is mostly less happy. Social workers in Scotland can and do offer throughcare to prisoners, but this is more likely if they already know the family. It is quite common, though, for Scottish social workers to be forbidden to hold short-term cases involving travel outside the county, which effectively puts a stop to work with prisoners. Social workers in the rest of the U K may offer a full throughcare service, particularly where a client is already well known to them, but the normal practice is for probation officers to take on this role.

At best, the field probation officer provides an extra means of communication between prisoners and their friends and families, drawing on experience of the ways in which people react to prison in order to reassure and inform people outside. Support is also offered to the prisoner, in carrying messages, in helping to find accommodation and employment and generally assisting with resettlement on release where necessary, and simply by being reliable in keeping in touch during the sentence. Prisoners' families are helped with the shock of the crisis when someone is first imprisoned, and given information about visiting and financial arrangements. The probation officer remains prepared to resist judging a person by the offence that led to imprisonment, while being prepared to confront offenders about the consequences of their behaviour on themselves, their loved ones, and the victims. In some cases, it is possible for officers to discuss prisoners' offending with them during the sentence, with a view to encouraging planning for the future. This is only applicable to a minority, however, because the prisoners are primarily interested in dealing with practical problems and the prison is an artificial environment in which to try to tackle deep-rooted patterns of offending. In any event,

> this whole approach rests on an individualized view of crime, which locates the reason for the client's imprisonment in personal inadequacy - a perspective which many probation officers and most clients would reject (Walker & Beaumont, 1981).

During the worst parts of a sentence, when a prisoner is extremely depressed, probation officers can try to offer encouragement and a link with the outside. Many officers feel that all they can really do is assist in minimising the damage done by a sentence of imprisonment, using their social work skills and training, and they are aware that even in this respect their potential contribution is limited.

It is often useful if probation officers can recruit volunteers from the prisoner's home town , because they can support members of the family and write to or visit isolated prisoners. Some prisoners value the natural, unpaid assistance given by a volunteer far more highly than professional caring, and strong relationships build up between volunteers and prisoners, particularly those serving long sentences.

The role of the Probation Service in work with prisoners could be greater. There was a widespread view that the Home Office Statement of National Objectives and Priorities deliberately down-graded this work by suggesting that resources could be better used elsewhere, implying that once people go to prison, they are beyond rehabilitation. This cynical shifting of resources arose from a desire to relieve pressure on the prisons by making use of probation expertise. In this sense, probation officers have a very important part to play, in demonstrating their belief that people can change, that they do change for the better, and that they are not forgotten by the society which has incarcerated them. Otherwise, as John McCarthy (then - but no longer - a prison governor) wrote, the persistence of cynical attitudes to prisoners becomes 'a process of collusion, not only among those who work inside prisons but also between society and the prison system which maintains a "quiet society" by keeping trouble out of sight in a metaphorical dustbin' (McCarthy, 1981).

The dustbin analogy also suggests another role for probation officers: someone from outside the prison system who has access to it and is prepared to 'blow the whistle' if clients are abused. It may be that probation officers do not have a particularly good record of doing so, but it does happen and it is arguably part of their task, although it is difficult to be sure that in taking up individual cases, one may not be setting the prisoner up for further victimisation. Consultation with colleagues experienced in prison work will usually be necessary in such situations. Some prisoners do feel that they are more vulnerable if nobody from outside is involved with them, as prisoners' autobiographies clearly show, so this can be a helpful role for probation work with imprisoned clients.

At worst, probation officers collude with the system by failing to insist on minimum standards of treatment of their imprisoned clients. More commonly, they accept that they can manage their workload by giving a low priority to throughcare work: after all, prisoners don't call in at their offices to remind them of unkept promises!

It may be that field probation officers should concentrate, in their work with prisoners, on mitigating the damaging effects of imprisonment. Raban, who has worked as a prison and as a field probation officer, suggests that there may be a way to improve throughcare work without waiting for prison probation officers' withdrawal from working inside the prisons. He argues that priority should be given to two main areas of work, 'sustaining and developing community links with the prisoner' and 'confirming the prisoner's individuality' (Raban, 1987). These are at least tasks which in most cases could be easily defined, in consultation with the prisoner. The strategy aims at keeping the home community alive in the prisoner's mind (although, as we saw in the previous chapter, there may be good reasons for prisoners to resist this if they are serving long sentences). To do it effectively, it would need to be far easier than it is at present for field probation officers to work in collaboration with prison officers in institutions running a 'personal officer' scheme.

PRISON-BASED PROBATION OFFICERS

Prison probation officers are seconded by the local Probation Service to work in prisons, usually on a fixed-term basis. (This is because of the real danger that they would otherwise become incorporated into the prison's way of doing things, and give a higher priority to serving its purposes than their role as a probation officer should allow). They are in an anomalous position in that they are answerable both to the prison governor and to the chief probation officer.

Much of what has been written about prison probation officers has concentrated upon the negative aspects of their work. For example, when their tasks were originally described, there were 21, of which only four related to the after-care of prisoners (Home Office Circular 241/1965). Although the details are out of date, this analysis is still applicable. This led to what Priestley has called 'role strain', in that it is not only difficult to satisfy two very different managers, it is harder still to convince prisoners of their caring orientation when some of the daily work carried out makes prisoners view the prison probation officer as 'a rather impotent acolyte of the system they despise'(Priestley, 1972).

This is borne out by prisoners' own accounts. Jimmy Boyle wrote that 'there is the odd guy who will go to the welfare officer, but most guys have no confidence in him and see him as a screw without a uniform' (Boyle, 1977)

Describing his own prison social worker (the Scottish term), he later wrote that 'He's a rather placid guy and carries keys to lock and unlock doors. In many ways he seems like a prison officer, the better type perhaps. I find this sort of meeting has little value' (Boyle, 1985).

Clearly, anyone in the prison who carries keys has a long way to go before gaining the trust of many prisoners, and this is the more true when civilian workers spend much of their time working alongside uniformed staff.

One way in which prison-based probation officers have tried to resolve this conflict has been to encourage shared working schemes with uniformed staff, of which more later. Another, related strategy has been to try to withdraw from 'welfare' types of work (making telephone calls for prisoners to find out why they have stopped getting letters, for example) and to work at greater depth with only selected prisoners. The size of caseload carried by most prison probation officers in any case prevents them from working with more than a minority of the prisoners for whom they are nominally responsible. In some prisons, groupwork is used, maximising staff resources. Such groups can be offence-centred (although there are obvious dangers about identifying some types of offender by inviting them to a group) and there is scope for joint groupwork with prison psychologists. Others are concerned with people at a particular stage of their sentence (such as pre-release groups and new lifers' courses) and can be run with education officers. In a few prisons, the spiritual dimension has been acknowledged by involving chaplains in groupwork.

Unfortunately, some prison-based probation officers do avoid conflict by going over to the institutional way of looking at things. One reason for the adoption by the National Association of Probation Officers of a policy that prison probation officers should be withdrawn in order to work instead from community teams, was a widespread feeling that many of them became infected by the prison environment, so that they worked in a less caring way and were cynical about clients (see Chapter One).

The NAPO policy, adopted in 1981, was partly born of a view that 'probation officers had overestimated their ability to achieve change in the prison system from a position inside the prison' (NAPO, 1987), and that more would be achieved by similar numbers of probation officers working with prisoners from an outside base. This begged the question of whether the Home Office would provide finance for such a service on the same basis as the prison-based one, and negotiations began with the Prison Officers' Association to ensure that no jobs would be lost as a result of the implementation of the policy. In the event, it has not been implemented, but there has been a considerable growth in joint working between prison officers and probation officers, in recognition that this is a necessary precursor to such a move. Recent Home Office interest in privatising some work with prisoners may be an incidental consequence of the debate about probation officers' withdrawal having taken place (Home Office, 1990).

The prison probation officer's work with individuals is carried out with great professionalism despite the considerable constraints imposed upon probation officers in some prisons. There is an important role for all civilian staff in prisons, in trying to help prisoners feel respected and valued as individuals, and in offering them ways of keeping up their links with the outside and their skills in dealing with everyday problems. Inevitably, however, the problems caused by institutionalisation will also be presented, and it would be inhumane to ignore them. Raban suggests that once probation officers withdrew,

The institution would be responsible for
  (a) the day-to-day welfare of inmates;
  (b) assistance in maintaining and developing survival skills which assist prisoners on release;
  (c) ensuring that there are effective channels of communication between the prisoner and family, friends and community agencies (Raban, 1987).

He goes on to assert that the potential for such a development has been demonstrated by the success of some joint working schemes and of social skills courses. The fact is, however, that the three tasks he identifies would be likely to come very low on the list of institutional priorities, and would not make it onto the core task list of most establishments. While these tasks are being performed effectively with some prisoners at present, the likelihood is that the proportion of prisoners to benefit from such help would diminish, especially at times when security was given higher priority   The NAPO proposal needs further development before it is attainable in practice.

It is very important, in the mean time, that field and prison-based probation officers develop more effective ways of communicating. There is considerable tension between the two wings of the probation service at present, partly because field officers tend to have less understanding of the issues outlined in the previous chapter. Field officers should more often incorporate a discussion with their prison-based colleague in their plans when visiting or reporting on prisoners, and there should be far more emphasis on this kind of liaison in probation officers' training.

PRISON OFFICERS

Many prisoners are prepared to talk to prison officers and to civilian instructors about their problems. A significant number of prisoners interviewed, reported doing so (Shaw, 1974; McDougall, 1980). It is worth noting that these studies were not looking at the take-up of welfare services offered by uniformed staff under joint working arrangements: the prisoners questioned were in a minority in being prepared to discuss their problems with anyone in the prison, but a significant minority did so with uniformed staff. Of course, particularly where there is no tradition of joint work, this raises questions about the training and support received by prison officers to work with prisoners' personal problems.

In some institutions, the staff culture means that it is not done openly, and in others that it is not done at all. For most prisoners, it is out of the question to trust a member of the uniformed staff with sensitive information of any kind: to do so risks compromising other prisoners, and thus breaching the inmate code, or is seen as jeopardising the prisoner's own position because prison officers are not trusted to keep it to themselves.

But prison officers may have more in common with inmates than many of the other staff, at least in terms of class, background and attitudes. They are likely to know individual prisoners far better than most of the other people who work with them, and to spend very much more time with them. Their jobs provide numerous opportunities for helping prisoners, be it a matter of advising on legal aid or bail (normally a specialist prison officer's job), helping an individual negotiate the rules for obtaining privileges, or simply talking something over. The prisons cannot run without a degree of cooperation between staff and inmates, and this exists largely because of such relationships of mutual respect. It would be easy - but rather arrogant - for other people working with prisoners to forget all this. Prison officers are not a homogeneous mass of uncaring turnkeys, and many prisoners recognise this, perhaps particularly in the dispersal prisons.

In recent years, it has become much easier for prison officers to develop specialised skills in what they tend to call 'welfare' work (the prison probation officer was called a welfare officer until the early 1970s). Many prisons have well-established schemes for joint working between probation officers and uniformed staff. A number of different models of joint work have been developed, varying according to prison regimes (Jepson & Elliott, 1985).

The trend towards joint work was given official endorsement in Home Office guidance on throughcare issued from 1986, which stressed the need for work involving prisoners' welfare to be shared between prison officers, probation officers and the other specialist staff, (C I 125/1986 for adults and C I 40/1988 for young offenders). It was also suggested that the Fresh Start changes in prison officers' working practices would release resources to allow prison officers to spend more time on such work (Home Office, 1988), although this was greeted sceptically by the POA in many prisons.

Prison officers have also reacted unfavourably to the idea of being given new duties without receiving adequate training - or indeed, any training at all in some institutions (see for example Lowe, 1989; Evans et al, 1988). However, where training has been carefully planned and has involved time outside the prison to observe other ways of working with young offenders, it has been regarded as a success (Shaw, 1984).

There is some evidence that welfare work has a low status among prison officers, whose culture may rather encourage more macho tasks, but Shaw suggests that this can be broken down over a period of time (Shaw, 1984). What may prove more difficult is to get prison officers to work with clients on offending behaviour, for which they receive no preparation or training. The experimental schemes seem to have avoided this area (Bottomley & Liebling, 1989; Lowe, 1989).

Prisoners who are prepared to use a welfare service provided by uniformed staff find them easier to get hold of than probation officers, though not always as helpful when they do see them (Evans et al, 1988).

Shared working has not always been adequately explained to the main-grade prison officers who are meant to make it work. Given extra time to carry out welfare duties, many prison officers have used it to get on with paperwork, writing institutional reports without necessarily seeing the prisoners concerned (Lowe, 1989).

Another problem, as might be expected, has been continuity: the welfare task is rarely given sufficiently high priority by prison managements to avoid the officers concerned being detailed to carry out other duties at short notice when staff are sick or on holiday (Chaplin, 1985). Naturally, this tends to disrupt the work of such officers and their relationships with the prisoners concerned.

The evidence about prisoners' willingness to engage with a welfare service provided by prison officers is mixed. The probation officer who set up the Leicester scheme described reluctant clients as 'a minority of inmates' (Shaw, 1984). The researchers who reviewed the experimental schemes found that the percentage varied according to the regime (more than half of those in detention centres preferred to keep their problems to themselves, whereas more than two-thirds of people interviewed in Youth Custody Centres - the precursors of YOIs - 'said they would take their problems to personal officers or another discipline officer' (Bottomley & Liebling, 1989). When adult prisoners are asked for their opinion, it is clear that more than a small minority object in principle to the idea of discussing their welfare problems with members of the uniformed staff, and in some cases the screening of clients by uniformed staff before they can see a probation officer may have been imposed in response to this consumer resistance (see Nash, 1988). This seems to have led to fewer applications for assistance - possibly a disproportionate reduction in applications by black prisoners (Wiseman, 1990).

Prisoners give a number of reasons for distrusting prison officers in the welfare role. The obvious one is that there is bound to be some hostility between captives and their custodians.

Prison officers respect this, and they do not generally like to force their concern upon unwilling recipients. To this extent, the 'screening' system, whereby all applicants for welfare assistance are seen first by a prison officer, would seem rather self-defeating.

Some prisoners, however, reject the notion of compromise in this matter completely. As one long-term man, asked about a shared working (SWIP) scheme, put it:

> No, I don't like talking to them. Not at all. 'Cause they're a prison officer, and they're not interested in your welfare, all they're interested in is keeping you under control and locked up, and when it comes to you telling them about your personal problems, I ain't gonna do that, you know.[...] when it boils right down to it, you don't go and tell your worst enemy your problems, do you?

This reservation is not taken particularly seriously in the literature reviewing the progress of shared working schemes. A major criterion of the success of the schemes has been their contribution to the regime in the prison concerned. Here again, there is conflicting evidence, although the writers concerned mostly feel positive about the impact of shared working on staff morale. Jepson & Elliott noted that 'appreciation by prison and probation staff of each other's skills had been heightened and co-operation improved' (Jepson & Elliott, 1986). Nash noted that once the probation officers moved on from a rather snooty view that shared working would release them from mundane work for 'the professional task as befits our training', and moved on to 'work with prisoners on their offences and criminal behaviour' this met with general approval and co-operation (Nash, 1988). He concludes that

> liaison between prison and probation officers has increased, and prison officers are now much more aware of individual prisoners' circumstances. There have been many contributions to the relaxed climate at Albany and I have no doubt that shared working is now one of them.

Elsewhere, however, probation officers in the field remain reluctant to share information about their clients with prison officers, and 'the main obstacle to shared working was the degree of prejudice and negative attitudes on both sides' (Bottomley & Liebling, 1989).

Prison officers are bound to feel that probation officers are trying to tell them how they could do their job better, and to offload menial work. Meanwhile, the probation officers experience discomfort because of feelings that they are relinquishing their proper responsibility for the welfare of prisoners, and may even fear that they are doing themselves out of a job. Their respective roles make such conflicts and discomfort inevitable (McDougall, 1984).

GOVERNORS

For a period, Borstal housemasters (who subsequently became Assistant Governors, then G5s) were explicitly expected to undertake 'social work duties' (Lowson, 1970). Many of these staff subsequently became governors of institutions. Just as it is incorrect to assume that all uniformed staff wish to avoid personal and constructive contacts with prisoners, it is untrue that helpful, caring approaches - even friendship or counselling in some cases - never occur between governors and prisoners. The senior member of the uniformed staff on each wing in a dispersal prison often knows the longer-term residents of the wing very well indeed, and may have become involved in helping with personal problems. With long-term prisoners, the governor of the institution can become similarly involved, not least because of intractable discipline problems with some inmates. Many who would not consider discussing problems with uniformed staff will talk to a governor who makes time available.

PSYCHOLOGISTS

Like many of the other staff with welfare responsibilities, prison-based psychologists can call on the resources of their colleagues in the field. In their case, this does not normally involve asking outside colleagues to make home visits (as a chaplain or probation officer frequently does), but rather to obtain professional support for their work and opportunities to keep up with developments. This seems to give psychologists a greater confidence in their independent professionalism than perhaps many prison probation officers have.

For career reasons, psychologists in prisons are often young and mobile, as compared to probation officers or chaplains. This affects their attitudes: they are unlikely to be as institutionalised as some of the other workers.

In addition to their work with individuals and groups of prisoners, they have a number of other functions. They are involved to some extent in staff selection and training, including training staff to run groups, and running courses on such issues as negotiating with hostage-takers. They carry out management consultancy for governors, and help with regime design. They undertake research, and have considerable autonomy in pursuing such interests. This includes evaluation of treatments, but also of regimes. They are responsible for collection of data which are translated into prison statistics, and sometimes for producing evidence and arguments for governor-grade staff planning changes. What follows will concentrate, however, upon psychologists' various roles in working with individual prisoners.

Psychologists work in teams, but they are few in number, so they tend to be concentrated in larger prisons, with each having some responsibilities in other institutions (although in Scotland, matters are organised differently: clinical psychologists are employed by the NHS and some specialise in prison work).

Psychologists are involved in both assessment and treatment. They write reports for courts, the Parole Board and various internal prison boards. This does not necessarily involve the use of psychological testing, but where such 'scientific' methods are used, efforts are made to ensure that the test instruments are not culturally biased. At some institutions (for example, some Young Offender Institutions) assessment work would take up a larger proportion of the working day than treatment. This can include keeping track of any changes in individuals after they receive treatment or training, which is on the borderline between research, assessment, treatment and regime design.

Treatment is readily available to individuals assessed as needing it. Most referrals are seen within seven days (which compares favourably with the availability of psychological services to people in the outside community in some parts of the country). It may involve membership of a group, and often has a training element (for example, social skills groups, relaxation therapy, anger control, drug and alcohol counselling).

Much treatment is aimed at mitigating the effects of imprisonment, and giving individual prisoners encouragement and opportunities to be positive about themselves. As with the other professionals in a prison setting, the clientele is partly self-selected, and some individuals take up a disproportionate amount of time. While interpreters are available when needed, it does appear that prisoners who cannot speak English are more difficult to treat and possibly less likely to receive treatment from psychologists than others.

A growing area is work with prisoners with HIV and AIDS. Clients are counselled about whether or not to have a seropositivity test, and helped to deal with the implications if they are tested. Such counselling has not always been made available, because of the mistaken belief of some governors and prison medical officers that AIDS is 'purely a medical problem' (Curran, 1987), and indeed there is evidence that prisoners have been dealt with in a very insensitive manner (McKeganey, 1990). However, it is clearly important that people with AIDS - in prison as elsewhere - are given support, and the encouragement to adopt a positive attitude and a healthy lifestyle, which may prolong their lives. A multi-disciplinary approach is needed if such a strategy is to have any chance in a prison environment (Curran, 1987), and this would help to involve outsiders in work with prisoners, as it has done with the Scottish AIDS Monitor buddy scheme.

Because of their experience of running groups in a prison environment, psychologists often co-operate with probation officers to design groups and courses. They try to co-ordinate provision by the medical and other services in order to prevent overlaps and manipulation by individuals.

Like other treatment staff, they have no formal responsibility to provide services for their uniformed or other colleagues, but this does not stop people coming to them. In some institutions, they provide courses on topics like occupational stress, in order to make an organised response.

There is considerable scope for joint work by chaplaincy and probation staff with prison psychology departments, and this is common. Although there might be some organisational problems if large numbers of field probation officers were to start making enquiries of psychologists, there may be scope for more liaison in the interests of individual prisoners. Some of the behavioural methods used are likely to be beyond the repertoire of other workers (for example, behaviourist therapies used subject to a contract with sexual offenders) but it is clearly desirable that probation officers understand both the theory being employed and the reasons for using particular treatments, so that they can reinforce the psychologist's work where appropriate (McGurk et al, 1987).

CHAPLAINS

The prison chaplaincy service has a long tradition: in the early days, chaplains were second in importance only to governors and medical officers. In some ways, this gives prison chaplains an ambiguous role which they can at times exploit for the benefit of individuals under their care.

Their status allows them a unique opportunity to obtain an overview of the mood of a prison. They sit on committees and boards at all levels in the institutional hierarchy, and they are required to see all prisoners on reception, all those who are placed in the punishment block, and everyone in the hospital.

Some chaplains are undoubtedly powerful figures, although many members of the uniformed staff would like to see their role increasingly marginalised (but like other civilian staff, chaplains find that uniformed staff are willing to approach them for help with personal problems). Key roles include membership of suicide prevention groups and race relations committees: where these functions are taken seriously by the institution's management, chaplains can have influence on the regime.

The training of chaplains now being appointed recognises the validity of 'clinical theology', which means that many chaplains see themselves as counsellors. Like the probation staff, most chaplains see their role not as offering false consolation or distractions for prisoners, but as having time for people who are in a difficult situation, encouraging them to accept the reality of their position and helping them to limit the damage.

Welfare needs which become apparent when prisoners are interviewed on their reception at a prison, may be shared out between the chaplain and the probation officer. For example, the probation officer or the chaplain might arrange for a 'field' colleague to visit the wife of a worried prisoner and report back.

In general, however, chaplains seem less likely to favour the 'outreach' model of working, because their duties tie them to set tasks; the daily visits to particular groups of prisoners, interviews in their offices on a call-up basis, and other routines. Like other helping professionals they can only engage with a minority of potential clients. The outsider might expect chaplains to be particularly involved in issues of guilt and work on avoiding reoffending, but in practice this would appear to be just as patchy as with other workers. Work with 'convenience' Christians undoubtedly offers opportunities to engage with such issues, and some chaplains are also willing to confront issues concerning male oppression - from which everyone in a male prison suffers, along with many victims of offences. There are frequent and important opportunities to work on prisoners' guilt and confusion about relationships with women. Many chaplains see this question of reconciliation of offenders with themselves and others as the central task of their ministry (Atherton, 1987).

Like prison probation officers, chaplains can call upon voluntary helpers. 'Chaplaincy visiting ministers' attend to the religious needs of prisoners belonging to minority groups, and have individual relationships with prisoners under the chaplain's direction.

Prison chaplains are almost exclusively male, but women are gradually being appointed to full-time posts. The vast majority of prison chaplains are white, however, with no black Catholic chaplains and very small numbers of black Methodist and Anglican chaplains at the time of writing (Tarleton, 1989). Each prison has to have a Catholic, an Anglican and a Methodist chaplain (not necessarily all full-time), and the Anglican chaplain is usually responsible for facilitating the practice of all other religions. The right of all prisoners to practise their religion is taken extremely seriously, although the degree of knowledge of comparative religion naturally varies between chaplains, as does the extent to which they are willing to cater for less orthodox needs. Courses are run centrally, to help increase chaplains' awareness of other faiths. Where appropriate, the chaplain can arrange to pay the travelling expenses of visiting ministers. Prisoners may, however, need to be quite insistent in asserting their religious rights.

The major religions seem to be recognised, although there is a continuing argument about the legitimacy of Rastafarianism. The Anglican Chaplain General has issued guidelines about religious practices and how these can be facilitated in prison, including hand-outs for officers escorting prisoners to weddings and funerals (Prison Service Chaplaincy, 1988). When prisons have to cope with religious demands on kitchens etcetera, prisoners have difficulties. For example, it is quite common for Moslems to be given a vegetarian diet as a 'short cut' which falls some way short of satisfying the requirements of their religious observation, and in most prisons there is no way of obtaining Halal meat (although this is under review by the Prison Department). Similarly, it is not regarded as practical to accede to the requirements of Vegan Buddhists for clothing and footwear not made of animal products. No special arrangements are made for the hygienic requirements of Sikh prisoners, and in some prisons the Sikh comb is banned on security grounds (although a miniature ceremonial dagger is now allowed). There is a long way to go before the needs of prisoners not fluent in English are effectively met (Prison Reform Trust, 1989).

Like other civilian staff, chaplains feel that their autonomy in prison work is protected by their joint accountability to the bishop and the prison governor. Also like the others, they are in danger of feeling very marginalised - which could be used to undermine their work where they were felt to be unsympathetic to a particular regime. Not unnaturally, this makes chaplains selective about the issues they take up with the management of an institution. In another sense, prison chaplains have to make a choice about the approach they take. The notion of Original Sin (that is, the idea that humans are inherently bad) was influential in prison design, and this persists in many details of prisons' regimes and conditions. There is an argument that this concept takes away from the individual the responsibility to do and to be good. Some chaplains feel that they can resist this influence and work in prisons towards their own liberation, and towards helping other people to change themselves. The prison environment in this sense provides unusual opportunities for in-depth work with individuals who acknowledge the need for change - and perhaps unusually, an opportunity to set the agenda for institutional change.

It would be a mistake for other civilian staff to ignore the potential for productive co-operation with chaplains, in the interests of prisoners.

As in so many other areas, however, the service provided varies widely according to the type of prison. Most prisoners in Category A and B (higher security) prisons do not have ready access to chaplains, and have to make appointments which are sifted by uniformed officers on their wings. While the dietary and religious needs of long-term prisoners in, for example, dispersal prisons are comparatively well catered-for, this is less likely to be the case in local prisons, where the civilian staff will also be less likely to have the time or opportunity to take up the needs of individual prisoners, who change daily.

Liaison

It is a truism that all the workers mentioned in this chapter need to liaise effectively with each other in the interests of their clients. This is easy to say, but often hard to do. There are bureaucratic barriers - it can be hard even for the different people to get hold of each other - and institutional constraints. There may be interprofessional rivalries or disputes which prevent clear communication. Nevertheless, the interests of the client are at stake, and ways need to be found to get around these problems.

Some staff feel that prisoners are mostly highly manipulative people who will often play one worker off against another to get what they want. In fact, prisoners serving long sentences may make contact with all the civilian services in the prison as a kind of pastime (the coping strategy known as 'gleaning': see above). There are also circumstances where the responsibilities of different types of staff overlap, and liaison then becomes important because there is a need to avoid 'mixed messages'. For example, if a psychologist is working with a prisoner on a social skills training programme aimed at improving his self-esteem, it will be counter-productive for a chaplain to make a simultaneous effort to get him to focus on his feelings of guilt about offending. Such clashes can only really be avoided by fairly frequent discussions about individuals.

Such liaison becomes more complicated when some of the staff involved are based in the prison, and others outside. If anything, this makes it all the more important. Prisoners feel that they are being manipulated if they are not told what is being done on their behalf. The importance of keeping them informed about things with which they have asked for help cannot be overstated. Of the groups of staff considered above, this situation arises most frequently with chaplains and probation officers. To take the latter as an example, there is a need for regular and habitual liaison between the field probation officer and the prison-based colleague. It needs to become habitual because that is a good way to avoid forgetting to liaise. There are some simple ways of getting into the habit... but the fact that they are simple has not meant that they have become at all widespread!

First, as we shall see in the next chapter, letters to prisoners are very important to them. This being so, it may be sensible for all typewritten letters to prisoners (which are usually the 'business' letters from probation officers in the field) to be copied and sent to the appropriate prison-based probation colleague.

Probation officers routinely record their work, without giving much thought to the reasons for doing so or the uses made of the records. There is a strong argument for making copies of the more reflective part of the record (the 'Part B' or quarterly assessment) available to colleagues within the Service who are working with the same client. There are bound to be concerns about the implications of this for the confidentiality of sensitive information, particularly when files have been one of the targets during prison riots in recent years. Good practice, however, is to share the information in such recording with the client, or in some cases to compile the assessment jointly with them.

When field probation officers visit prisoners, they do not often think to talk to their prison-based colleague. Although this may not be something to be done routinely - there is not the time - it is certainly valuable for field officers to meet the prison-based colleague concerned from time to time. It can be a useful way of finding out what is happening at the prison and what goes on in prisons generally. This will make for more informed discussions with individual prisoners. For field probation officers without prison experience, it would seem important to go further than such occasional discussions: most prison probation teams welcome lengthier visits from field colleagues, and there is a lot to be said for arranging to spend a week or two observing the work of a prison-based colleague. With the increase in shared working, some of these comments also apply to liaison with uniformed prison officers - provided it is with the client's active consent.

Finally, probation officers may wish to consider finding out the timetable for institutional review meetings. Some prisoners see these as a farcical routine, but others value the interest a few field probation officers show by attending them. In many cases, travelling long distances to attend frequent and largely trivial meetings would not be given a high priority. But they do offer an opportunity to feed information and opinions in at the level of those who work with the client day-to-day, and in situations where a prisoner faces a crisis at home, it can be very helpful to gain the support of such staff. For example, such a meeting might have considerable influence on a governor's decision about whether to let a young offender attend a relative's funeral, or whether to grant home leave before a death.

The Limits of Professional Power

It is in some ways a good thing that there are limitations upon the power of the professionals who work with prisoners. There are, however, institutional restrictions which are not in the interests of the prisoner.

There are circumstances, as in other kinds of work, where the battle for status and power takes precedence over the interests of prisoners in the minds of the people who work with them. For example, it could be argued that the underlying reason for the National Association of Probation Officers' policy of withdrawing probation officers from work inside prisons has to do with concern about their professional status. The interests of the clients are perhaps in danger of being forgotten in the quest for status. A less contentious example might be the tendency of workers in large bureaucracies to stand on their dignity in the face of any slight, real or imagined. Thus, disputes often occur between medical staff and other professionals in prisons, when those who are not qualified in medicine presume to make judgements about prisoners' mental condition.

In different ways, each of these examples shows how vulnerable prisoners are to the professional rivalries of prison staff.

The prison environment curbs the freedom of professional workers to practise according to their codes of ethics and their personal preferences. This can work both ways. Many of those who have commented on the Prison Medical Service have suggested that standards would be considerably improved if it were brought under NHS control. In practice, local NHS general practitioners *are* the Prison Medical Service in two-thirds of establishments (Chief Inspector, 1989) and they do not necessarily provide a high-grade service.

Social work values demand that clients be accorded the right of self-determination and the right to confidentiality, but these are systematically denied to prisoners, and probation officers working with them have to do so in the context of an environment which undermines clients' dignity and makes an equal relationship impossible. Prison doctors, similarly, face real ethical problems about confidentiality (particularly, in recent years, where the HIV virus and seropositive status are concerned) and about consent for treatment. Can a sexual offender who is offered drug treatment which will enhance his chances of early release give informed and truly voluntary consent?

The prison environment compromises professional ethics and preferences daily, and it is important for staff in prisons to have sufficient experience and confidence to deal with these conflicts. It is also important that the professionals working in prisons are experienced - not so much for the reasons often given, that they need to be able to withstand the manipulation of hardened criminals, but because experience is some protection against being compromised by the system.

While there is no doubt that probation officers, psychologists, doctors, teachers and chaplains have done a great deal to make prisons less inhumane places, they can all be locked out - individually or collectively - when the institution does not want them poking their noses in. The overriding imperative of prisons in this country is containment, security. Almost any professional activity can be prevented on 'security' grounds. All civilian staff working with prisoners have to bear this in mind, and field staff are well-advised to consult prison-based colleagues in advance about any activity they think might attract the interest of security staff. Educational classes frequently do not happen because uniformed staff needed to escort prisoners to them are required for more urgent duties. These 'security' demands are even put before taking prisoners for their court appearances, and although such attendance is their right, lawyers and magistrates have frequently been unsuccessful in forcing governors to respect it.

Such absolute power is open to abuse. The number of black workers in all areas of the criminal justice system is clear evidence of institutional racism: black people are so extremely under-represented (Alibhai, 1989) that they are commonly mistaken for defendants and treated accordingly. Black lawyers and probation officers tell similar stories of racist behaviour by other professionals and by their own colleagues. For example:

'Recently, at the beginning of his service, an officer visited a hostel in the Midlands with a potential white resident. On arrival the white warden immediately offered his hand to the offender and started to discuss the referral.'

'Last year a recently recruited female officer went to see the manager of a London probation project. She waited and waited to see the supervisor. The project worker had assumed that she was an applicant for a vacant cleaning job, which, the supervisor explained, was why she was kept waiting.'

'A female officer on her first day of new employment arrived at the office at the appropriate time. She was told that the supervisor was busy, later that the supervisor was unavailable and taking tea. Eventually the new officer confronted the receptionist. There were abject apologies all round. The officer had been mistaken for an offender.' (Fletcher, 1988)

Black and female lawyers and probation officers frequently find their credentials challenged in demeaning ways on 'security' grounds when visiting prisons - and at other times. To quote further examples:

'An officer was appointed to a team in London; he met his four white colleagues on arrival on his first day. Around lunchtime the same day he was stopped going through a door by a white officer who demanded to know where he was going. The white officer had failed to recognise the new colleague whom he had met just two hours earlier.'

'A newly-qualified female officer was visiting a prison in London. The visit had been arranged via the prison probation officer. Upon arrival she was refused admission to the prison. She produced her letter of appointment and other means of identification and was still refused admission. She called for the prison senior probation officer but he was unable to move matters forward. After complaining she was told that a black person had once tried to enter the prison posing as an officer. At the same time a white colleague visited another London prison without any means of identification other than a banker's card and was admitted without further question' (Fletcher, 1988).

The situation has been so difficult for black professionals that support groups have been formed - indeed, this was part of the purpose of the Association of Black Probation Officers when it was founded. In Fletcher's survey (on which this section has drawn heavily, simply because there has been so little written about this issue):

> All the black officers reported that the experience of racism coupled with a relative absence of any support or understanding from white colleagues was a frequent, almost daily experience [which] has led some black officers to leave the service (Fletcher, 1988).

The prison system has begun to respond to criticism of this kind. Since 1981, when the first Prison Department policy statement was issued (Circular Instruction 28/1981), developments have been quite rapid - in policy if not in practice. The 1981 policy was tentative, and viewed problems of racism as latent rather than actual, a matter for prison staff's professionalism, and very much a matter for training in 'awareness'. Two years later, a new policy acknowledged that 'Race relations is an issue which concerns us all' (C I 56/1983), and by 1986 ethnic monitoring had been introduced in response to evidence of discrimination in the allocation of prisoners to work, accommodation, sporting activities and so on, and disproportionate numbers of black people facing disciplinary charges. The 1986 policy also introduced mandatory appointment of Race Relations Liaison Officers at every prison - although there was no requirement to give such officers any systematic support - and the policy was further strengthened in 1991. In practice, however prison officers still see racism in prisons as unproblematic and feel that it is given too much attention by the hierarchy (Genders & Player, 1989).

Nonetheless, a County Court judgement in 1987 made it clear that complaints under the Race Relations Act would be accepted from prisoners, and governors have been told to take action to deal with offensive language by staff.

This does nothing to alter the everyday experience of black workers at the hands of prison staff. Throughout the 1970s and 1980s, evidence came to light of uniformed prison staff involvement in far-right organisations (Gordon, 1983), and less sensational examples of racist behaviour continue to surface, as in the examples quoted above.

Sexist comments are routine in male prisons, and rarely challenged. The occupational culture of prison officers produces a kind of contrived chivalry towards women staff and visitors, and in some institutions women civilian staff have had a battle to gain keys. Visitors may be sexually harassed, for example by strip searching or being asked to lift their arms when walking through security arches so that the shape of their breasts is exposed. Professional staff need to remain vigilant and prepared to challenge such discrimination.

People with disabilities - prisoners, staff and visitors - face particular obstacles in prisons. Access is difficult, and movement within most prisons is extremely hard for anyone in a wheelchair; indeed, many cells are too small to allow anyone in a wheelchair even to turn it. Since 1989, however, the Prison Department has been instructing its architects to pay attention to facilities for disabled people (a provision which has been legally required of other public buildings for many years), and matters should begin to improve as far as new and refurbished prisons are concerned (Masham, 1990).

4. How to work with Prisoners

What is helpful practice? In general, good practice in counselling relationships with prisoners relies upon the same skills and attitudes which are required in any other caring work.

There is no special mystique about working with prisoners - although it helps if the worker has at least an idea of what it is like to be a prisoner, and has some knowledge of the jargon used in prisons, so that there is no need to ask distracting questions during interviews (see Chapter Two).

Like anyone else seeking help, prisoners respond well to warm, reliable, genuine and understanding people who are prepared to set aside time to listen. The prison environment obviously imposes some constraints upon meeting these standards, but prisoners are generally understanding about these - as long as the worker does not seek to use them as an excuse for giving a less good service. (These issues were discussed in more detail at the end of Chapter One).

In this chapter, examples of helpful work with prisoners will be given, concentrating on specific situations like letters, telephone calls, visits, report-writing and assistance with planning for release. Some particular areas where helpful work is at present hampered by prison service and other institutions' policies will then be briefly considered.

LETTERS TO PRISONERS

There is plenty of evidence that letters are important to prisoners. Nobody who has seen the response to the arrival of the post on a wing could doubt it. Many spouses of prisoners are well aware of the importance of letters, and write frequently - but a minority of prisoners receive few letters. Getting letters does to some extent denote a prisoner's standing, and this should be taken more fully into account by people who work with them from outside.

Generally, we are more eager to receive personal communications than business ones. Thus, prisoners are less likely to be cheered up by a formal letter from their solicitor than by a chatty one from home. But, in keeping with their special circumstances, they are much less likely than people at liberty to throw mail away, even formal letters. This offers an opportunity, which does not always seem to be taken: if we know that letters are saved, even memorised, should we not write more carefully and more often than many field probation officers do to their clients in prison? It pays to remember that:

'Keeping letters in prison is almost a universal practice. They tend to be hoarded like rare commodities in any community and from time to time they are taken out and re-read to reassure oneself that someone on the outside really cares' (Grimsby, 1974).

The evidence is that handwritten letters are valued more greatly than typed ones, whoever sends them: 'Certainly a hand written letter dispersed among the others can add another humanising aspect occasionally, whatever our handwriting is like!' (Grimsey, 1974)

Occasionally, prisoners have actually made a point of asking me to write my letters rather than have them typed.

Given that prisoners spend a lot of time thinking about the meaning of their letters, it is important to write unhurriedly, and unambiguously. It is better to write that you have visited a prisoner's family and they were well, than to say that you visited a man's wife but she was out, or that something came up which you will need to discuss when next you meet. The chances are, his mind will prey on why the appointment was not kept, or what the mysterious matter for concern might be. Since we know that prisoners give their letters a lot of thought, they could be used more purposefully than at present by many probation officers, priests and voluntary workers. If there are issues which need discussion on a visit, a letter can suggest what these might be, so that the recipient has a chance to start sorting out what she or he wants to say.

Given what we also know about prisoners' changed perspectives of time (discussed in Chapter Two), it is important that letters are used to keep prisoners informed of progress on things they have written asking for help in doing. Prisoners interviewed about their letters have said that they prefer to be told by letter before they are visited, so that they can prepare mentally for the visit, and that they expect to be informed by letter of any changes to the arrangements for a visit (Williams, 1991). This is partly because they are not always told accurately who their visitor is, and they may arrive expecting a loved one or a solicitor, to find someone else waiting to see them, which is naturally frustrating. When prisoners write to somebody, they expect a response, and this should be given wherever possible by return of post, even if only by way of an acknowledgement and some idea of the timescale for giving a fuller reply, because prisoners need to retain some dignity and sense of involvement in solving problems: 'It's the not knowing [...]. You can't actually get there and do the things yourself, you've got to resort to other people to sort things out.'

In a system where it can be difficult to decide who to write to, due to shortage of cash for stamps, every letter deserves to be taken seriously. The literature on 'street-level bureaucracy' shows how frequently those in public service jobs fall into the trap off treating their clients' requests as routine, when to the individual they are unique and immediate (see for example Hughes, 1958, pp 54/5; Williams, 1991).

We have seen that prisoners sometimes withdraw from contact with the outside world. At such times they will not write or respond to letters - but this does not mean that outsiders should give up writing to them. It can, of course, be difficult to conduct a one-way correspondence, but it is important to try and keep the links open at times when the prisoner cannot. Sometimes, not writing is an expression, however small, of freedom of choice:

> There may be some fatalistic relief in reducing the emotional reliance upon outsiders. It increases the individual's autonomy; it ensures that the absence of visitors or letters is not a recurrent worry, and that such absences do not provide opportunities for patronizing sympathy by officers (Cohen and Taylor, 1972).

We need to respect this, but we do not violate it by keeping up our side of the correspondence unless specifically asked to stop writing.

Writing about prisoners serving short sentences, Corden found a direct correlation between the low number of letters and visits from probation officers received by some prisoners, and the likelihood that they would score 'high' on a scale measuring social isolation (Corden et al, 1978). Rather worryingly, this seems to suggest that probation officers may be making least contact with some of those most in need of help in retaining or finding accommodation.

Since the 1960s, when the notion of throughcare began to gain acceptance, it has been common ground in texts setting out good practice for probation officers that regular correspondence is desirable. Monger, for example, wrote that regular letters from field probation officers to prisoners demonstrated 'to the offender a continuing interest in his welfare' and served to 'keep open what have been described as the lifelines to the outside world' (Monger, 1967). Similar sentiments have been expressed in successive editions of *Jarvis's Probation Officer's Manual*. But in practice, officers are less conscientious about this.

Prisoners will not necessarily thank outsiders for routine or standardised letters. It may be a clever work-saving device to write a standard letter and have it sent to all imprisoned clients, but prisoners from the same town tend to share their news, and will soon spot what is happening. A purely formal letter is functional in some circumstances, but 'form' letters can be resented.

One prisoner said, 'I just kept getting letters from people saying that they were now my probation officer, and that they'd hope to see me soon. Nobody ever did, but I had five people say that they were.' Even allowing for the possibility of some exaggeration, this has a guiltily familiar ring! It shows how dangerous it is to make even vague promises in letters to prisoners without making a note of them and acting on them, and it also illustrates the annoyance caused by purely formal letters. Kingston's small-scale study found that 'probation officers made promises about visiting their clients which they then failed to keep', and she went on to suggest that 'if a contract framework of visits was established, then this would not only prevent the client having unfounded expectations, but would also help the probation officer to keep a track of his commitments' (Kingston, 1979).

While this may be idealistic, it would seem sensible for some discussion to take place in every case about how often visits are likely to be possible or necessary.

Should people working with prisoners share personal information? Is it appropriate to do so in letters? Opinions vary, but my own view is that the answer to both questions is Yes. But there is not much point giving information about oneself when no meeting with the client has taken place: giving such information by letter is bound to seem contrived. People generally share personal information in a more natural way than this, discussing topics as they come up. Counsellors normally do make some use of self, including judicious use of personal information. Grimsey suggests this can 'help a prisoner to become aware that he is not communicating only with an official but with a person and he is able to respond more as a whole person. As it happens I have twice found, over the years, that the mention of a bereavement in my family has evoked vivid concern and response which marked a turning point in our relationship' (Grimsey, 1974).

This may be constrained, in the case of some prisoners, by considerations of whether it is wise or safe to share certain information (such as the worker's home address or telephone number, or details of one's sexual orientation). The experience described, however, rings true, and discussion of personal troubles (while not allowing them to take over at the expense of the work with the prisoner) can be legitimate and give an opportunity for the inmate to put something into the relationship - the chance to help others is an unacknowledged need of many prisoners (see Chapter Two). It can go a long way to humanise an otherwise formal relationship and to build trust, if some personal information is shared. Where a hobby or interest is shared by volunteer or worker and prisoner, this can be helpful in a number of ways; discussion of a common interest can increase mutual trust and respect, making it easier to ask for help or advice in future, and can also make visits and letters more interesting.

Many people worry about whether they should mention certain things which are not normally readily available to the prisoner; drinking, outings and holidays. Experience suggests that as long as such issues are handled sensitively, they too can help to normalise and improve relationships. Having specifically asked how individuals felt about getting holiday postcards, my own practice is now to send them to everyone I know in prison because they have consistently said that far from upsetting them, this shows that someone is thinking about them even whilst enjoying a holiday. Similarly with discussions of socialising: it would be artificial to pretend that meals or parties did not involve drinking, and absurd to censor conversation on those grounds.

LIAISON BY TELEPHONE

It is often easier for probation officers, solicitors, ministers and friends to discuss prisoners over the telephone than by letter, but it can be frustrating trying to get hold of prison-based probation officers and chaplains. Secretarial support in prisons is often not as generous as in the field, and institutional regimes mean that workers have to be in certain places at certain times. Uniformed staff do not necessarily see it as a very high priority to track down 'civilian' colleagues for callers, although this varies considerably. Messages do not necessarily get through.

Nevertheless, some information has to be given by telephone. It is usually wise to follow it up with a letter or in person. For example, there is a requirement on court duty officers in most probation areas to follow carefully-worded instructions about anyone considered a suicide risk, and there are corresponding policies for prison officers. In such cases, the senior probation officer should be informed by telephone, and this should always be followed up in writing (for which most probation services have a standard form, kept in court files). Wherever possible, escorting prison officers should also be told personally. Their response may seem callous or indifferent, but they are aware of the additional responsibilities involved.

When is the best time to catch a prison probation officer or chaplain? Regimes and routines vary so much that it is impossible to generalise. However, in most cases, probation officers are likely to be in their offices first thing in the morning (until 9.30) and at the end of the day (after 4.00pm). In some prisons, where the switchboard is staffed by uniformed officers from late afternoon, it can be difficult to get through to civilian staff at that time. If one is told that there is nobody in the Probation Department or the Chaplaincy, it is worth trying an expression of surprise: 'That's odd, they've just been on the phone asking me to call straight back!' Prison probation officers get quite indignant about this habit of saying they've all gone home, but it is a practice which seems to persist. In many prisons, civilian staff take their lunch break at midday to fit in with institutional routines, which means it is often easier to get hold of them between 1.00 and 2.00 pm than at other times.

Prison-based colleagues work under different pressures to people outside, and may have different priorities. They will feel quite comfortable reminding their counterparts outside of things they have undertaken to do for clients, and one has to learn to take this with good grace. It is worth bearing in mind that the prisoner may be reminding the staff member of a request every day.

PRISON VISITS

What has been discussed under Letters applies equally to visits: there need be no areas of discussion which are necessarily taboo, though there is no need to talk about things which 'rub in' their predicament. Prison officers sometimes criticise female visitors (both personal and professional) for wearing 'provocative' clothes, but this is a matter of opinion. Most prisoners are glad to see visitors dressed attractively, not because this satisfies any sexual need but because it shows that they have taken trouble over their appearance. Indeed, any change from the institutional routine, including the chance to talk to anyone from the outside, is welcomed by many people in prison.

Even friendly visits need planning. There is so little time for visitors in most prisons that they need to work out in advance why they have come. Flexibility is needed, but prisoners appreciate purposeful discussions - and may prepare a mental agenda for visits themselves.

Some busy professionals leave the task of booking visits to a secretary, but this is unwise. It introduces scope for misunderstandings, and if there is any question about the booking on arrival at the prison, one is in a stronger position if one can truthfully say ' I know I'm booked in because I arranged it myself'. If it proves impossible to make a visit when planned, a telephoned or written explanation should be given to the prisoner, with some idea of when another visit is planned.

A prison visit is a conversation, but it is rather a strained one in many cases. It does not do to be too business-like at first, especially on the first visit to a prisoner. The prisoner is 'checking out' the visitor; how genuine is their interest? One way of dealing with these

79

concerns, after the initial social pleasantries, is to use Kingston's (1979) notion of a 'contract framework of visits'. This can be extended to a general discussion of ' How I like to work'. This has been a useful ice-breaker in many of my conversations with prisoners. For example, have you read the prisoner's file, or do you prefer to make your own mind up about people? Are you keeping records of your contacts, and are these open? How often do you plan to write and visit? Thus, one can communicate one's personal style and concern for the client's rights and welfare.

With experience, one learns how much of oneself to disclose, and when these boundaries can be crossed with exceptional individuals. A surprising number of professionals working with prisoners become friends with some of them. In general, though, there is a need for boundaries, as much to protect the prisoner as the worker. If a prisoner speaks of personal favours done by a chaplain, there is a danger that other staff will hold this against them, as an example of 'manipulative' behaviour or of favouritism by the worker concerned.

Like a visit to an acquaintance in hospital, prison visits can seem embarrassingly lengthy, with periodic silences. This is where planning comes in. If the visit is for a reason (however vague), there is likely to be less of a problem of how to spend the time. There is also nothing to stop a visitor leaving before the end of the time allotted, although some prisoners would be disappointed by this. Some prisoners view discussion of the world inside as depressing and likely to lead to them doing 'hard time', but others may be pleased that an outsider is interested in such details of their lives - this needs checking at the outset. Many people value news from home and local newspapers - but the rules about sending these vary.

Prisoners' lives do not change very much from day to day, and this can make it hard for them to feel they have very much to offer conversationally. Of course, it helps if there is some shared interest to fall back on. But visitors can also simply chat about their children, their pets, their car, their holidays or whatever. While there are those who would question the usefulness of professionals spending their time in such a way, the interest of a relatively intelligent outsider can be seen as a good thing in itself. Not every visit will be so inconsequential, and silences may have their uses too, but visits need not be uncomfortable. In the case of probation officers, unless they are talking to someone at the beginning of a long sentence, there is always the opportunity to encourage prisoners to review their plans on release (accommodation, work, relationships, finances) and the need to discuss their offending behaviour and the risks of reoffending.

While many prisoners may feel no guilt, or indeed proclaim their innocence, it is important to let them know that they do not need to suffer the corrosive effects of guilt alone. Sometimes a visit is not the place for such a discussion, but referral can appropriately be made to a prison psychologist, chaplain or probation officer for private discussion.

The visiting facilities accorded to professionals are often much better than ordinary visitors experience, and this includes the length of time allowed. Like many other interviews, there may be constraints upon the time available - but these can be self-imposed as well as ordained by the institution. If you only have an hour to spend at the prison because you have a long journey home, say so at the outset. Brief visits to a prisoner can be surprisingly constructive and purposeful. Sometimes, on travelling a long way, there is more than one prisoner to see. Particularly if you know the clients concerned, think carefully about the order in which to see them (although this may be taken out of your hands if the prisoners are not immediately available for interview). Will client X monopolise your time? Does client Y's problem need unhurried discussion?

In some cases it may be appropriate to use the extra visiting facilities to make it easier for family members to have a civilised visit. There is the possibility of special additional visits (organised in conjunction with the chaplain, a governor or the prison probation officer) in particular circumstances. But if a probation officer, solicitor or vicar is visiting a prisoner, why not bring another visitor along? This can sometimes be irksome, but it can also be a considerable help with the relationship with clients, and make a valuable insight into their personal situations, as well as making a link with contacts outside.

Because of the need for economy, probation officers often visit by the car-load. Old hands will know a good pub near the prison. How will the clients feel if their probation officers turn up after a good lunch, smelling of alcohol?

One of the most difficult matters arising from prison visits is the question of how to break bad news. We can learn a lot, in dealing with such situations, from the experience of prison chaplains, who are the people generally called upon to break the news to a prisoner when loved ones die. The following section is adapted from a training session for newly-appointed chaplains given by Rev. Tom Johns.

First of all, it is essential to know the full facts. In breaking the news of a death, there have been cases of malicious reports, and it is necessary to be absolutely sure that the news is true before passing it on. Bear in mind, too, that you may not be the first to bring the news: it could already have arrived on the grapevine or through the media, or in a 'Dear John' letter. This may mean that there will still be a reaction from the prisoner, and that it will be more extreme because for the first time an authority figure who knows is present. All this suggests that the normal visiting facilities may not be the best venue for breaking really bad news, and that the worker may wish to consider whether she or he is at any risk of personal aggression in doing so. Arrangements will readily be made by the prison authorities to provide a private place for a difficult interview - and this may be helpful for other reasons too, since people sometimes associate bad news with the place they heard it.

Certainly 'props' may be valuable on visits generally, and particularly where bad news has to be given; a box of tissues, cigarettes and matches (even if you don't smoke), a cup of tea. Experience suggests that it is best to get more or less straight to the point, rather than indulging your own nervousness and pussy-footing around.

Where a death is involved, prisoners sometimes value the offer to attend the funeral with them - but do not assume that the prison will allow them to go. Where close relatives are seriously ill, a brief home leave will sometimes be granted.

In giving bad news, the normal counselling skills of genuiness and accurate empathy are particularly needed. It is no use giving false consolation ('I know just how you feel' or 'everything will be fine' or 'Time is a great healer'). Being quiet with the client while the news sinks in, and offering to withdraw if there is a need for private reflection, will be remembered with gratitude in many cases. There is a particular need for liaison with prison-based staff when leaving someone with depressing things to think about: if there is any danger that the prisoner might attempt suicide or self-harm, or lash out at other people, the uniformed staff must be informed. Arrangements can then be made for them to be checked regularly.

Thoroughness in finding out the facts of the matter will also be appreciated. The natural response is to ask questions. Some of them will be unanswerable but it can help to put people's minds at rest if you have established the answers to others: how did a person die, at what time, what are the funeral arrangements, how did other key people react, who else has been told?

Such news is often not a complete surprise, as in many bereavements and marital breakdowns. It can help the person to put the news in context if they are gently invited to talk about what has led up to it. The possibilities of ongoing help and referral to other helping individuals need to be introduced before the end of the visit. Small gestures also mean a lot when people have had shocking news: sympathy cards to the prisoner and any relevant family members, for example - and it is worth bearing in mind how absurdly hard it can be for a prisoner to send flowers or even a card. It is worth involving the prison probation officer or chaplain at an early stage with such problems.

It is important, too, not to be judgemental about people's reaction to bad news. Prisoners do seem to become more introspective and look at things more in terms of the implications for them. This is partly imposed by their environment. It is also worth remembering what many people who have not worked with serious offenders find surprising: the death of a victim can be grieved as keenly and genuinely as any other bereavement.

Such news will often have long-term implications, but the period immediately after hearing it is not necessarily a good time to discuss these. Another visit may be needed for such discussion.

Where one is the originator of bad news (for example, refusal to recommend parole), it is hard also to be the counsellor offering sympathy. It may be important to be the one who gives the news, 'owning' the decision, and then necessary to back off and let someone else offer support - perhaps setting this up in advance.

One needs to be calm, unhurried, well informed, and to liaise effectively with the other people involved. If you can manage this, it is much easier than otherwise to pass on unwelcome news. If you are genuinely upset about the news, say so. In extreme situations, some people do need to be comforted physically. If you can do this with real feeling, do so - but warn the uniformed staff on duty first. If you are not comfortable with the idea, prepare yourself - and be careful not to start back if the client comes toward you for comfort. Consider touching the client's arm or in some similar way showing compassion while limiting the degree of physical contact involved.

FORMAL REPORT-WRITING

A common complaint by prisoners is that reports are prepared when they are considered for parole, on the basis of limited contact by people who hardly know them. In some cases, this is partly because local Probation Service policy discourages officers from visiting prisoners until they are being reviewed for parole, by which time it is too late to build up much of a relationship before the report is due. [Such local policies clash with the spirit of the National Position Statement agreed by the Association of Chief Officers of Probation, (ACOP, 1990).]

In order to make a case for a prisoner to be released early on parole, a report writer needs to able to work from a position of having formed a relationship with the person and gained a good degree of knowledge about the circumstances of the case. The reports by outside agencies will, otherwise, be discredited or at best regarded as less helpful than those written by people inside the prison. Although technically a probation officer is asked to describe the prisoner's 'home circumstances' if released, field probation officers' reports in practice contain recommendations and, as the ACOP document suggests, some idea of the basis of knowledge on which they were written, and of the work that would be undertaken by the supervising officer if the prisoner were to be released.

Coker and Martin surveyed Probation Services about their policies on contact with life-sentence prisoners (noting Cohen and Taylor's finding that prisoners' hope for the future was easier to keep alive if it is non-specific, that is, not fixed on a particular prospective release date). They found that fifty percent of the Probation Service allocated a probation officer to a lifer before a release date was fixed. They also interviewed probation officers, and over a third of them felt that earlier involvement than theirs would have been good practice. But Coker and Martin's interviews with prisoner suggest that such intervention would be rejected as paternalistic and inappropriate, offering intangible counselling rather than the concrete help they wanted upon release.

A more recent small-scale study found that while six of a sample of sixteen prisoners (not all lifers) agreed that early contact from a probation officer would have been unwelcome to them, they were outnumbered by seven who had valued early contact or would have wished it (Williams, 1990). Several of the men interviewed made the point that a field probation officer's familiarity with them could lead to a more plausible parole report: 'they should keep in touch regularly. So that by the time I am up for parole, and things like that, they know, y'know, everything about me.'

Indeed the probation officer's involvement over a substantial period was seen as part of the service's raison d'etre by one:

> In my case it was helpful to me to have early contact with him because he's then, he's now able to see the difference between me now and then which is so important for release: if you're no different from when you came in, you're a risk.

Only one of those interviewed made reference to anything like a contractual relationship. In doing so, he described what might be taken as a model of good practice for work with long-term prisoners, based upon a realistic approach to their chances of parole and upon a negotiated working arrangement with the client. He said his probation officer:

> goes to great pains to explain that he's trying to build up a case at this stage so that like perhaps in the last year or two we can look at something [...] At least he does try and encourage you that there is a chance [...] we've discussed the parole situation, and he's working towards getting me sort of 18 months, 20 months at the end of me sentence.

Logically, this is the sort of relationship that probation officers would need to have with clients serving long sentences if they were to be in a position to write 'home circumstances' reports which were helpful both to the prison and the prisoner. It can only exist where the resources are made available for meaningful throughcare contact before the report is requested. As Monger put it:

> After-care it is suggested, is a misnomer which has been literally interpreted and which has done far more harm than good. To the offender, any helper who arrives on the scene after sentence is all over, arrives at precisely the time when he wants help least (Monger et al, 1981).

How much more true this must be of the long-term prisoner than the petty recidivist offenders interviewed for Monger's study.

Not surprisingly, when some clients are interviewed for parole reports at a late stage, they feel that their case has not been done full justice.

Just as it is regarded as unprofessional for probation officers to reproduce large chunks of old reports when preparing new ones for the court (but it happens), it is clearly unacceptable to regurgitate unchecked or possibly out-of-date material from a prisoner's file when preparing a parole report (but it happens). Again, what follows is an attempt to describe best practice, disregarding local resourcing problems.

While clients are entitled by law to a copy of their court report, the status of parole reports is ambiguous. They seem, legally, to be the property of the body for which they are prepared, and there is no consensus about sharing their contents with their subjects. It seems to me that natural justice demands that we do so, and it is certainly normal practice for many probation officers. However the prison staff do not expect it, and many prison staff do not divulge the detailed contents of their reports. This makes it difficult, and probably counterproductive, to give clients copies of the reports prepared by the probation officers. In those circumstances, the best that can be achieved is to go through a draft of the report with a prisoner. This has the advantage of preserving the anonymity of any third parties who may have given prejudicial information, although the ethics of this are debatable.

Realistically, if the inmate is to have any chance of influencing the contents of a probation officer's report, this means either preparing a draft after an earlier visit, or making two visits. The latter course of action may well lead to problems with line managers about travel costs, so there is a lot to be said for trying to calculate when a report is due, and starting work in anticipation of the request. While much of the information will be gleaned from records, at least the subject gets a chance to check it.

The timetable for writing parole reports should allow for liaison with other workers. At the very least, the field probation officer and prison probation officer should try to 'get their acts together'. They may not always agree , but they will look foolish if their reports contradict one another outright, and both may benefit from spending some time on consultation. The credibility of field officers' reports is greatly enhanced by evidence that they have investigated the subject's behaviour during the sentence and discussed the recommendation with colleagues in the prison. Ideally, this process would include a face to face meeting, perhaps after a visit, but this is difficult to arrange in practice.

It is also important to avoid glaring contradictions between parole reports and previous court reports, which form part of the same dossier. If a colleague's previous report suggests or states that an inmate is a poor risk for community supervision, it is essential to address what has changed since then if parole is now being recommended.

In recent years, there has been a tendency to try to replace formal reports with single-page forms where the report writer is invited to tick boxes. In practice, except where the presumption is in favour of parole (as in the case of many young offenders and those serving short sentences), such 'reports' have little influence. If it is to be a persuasive document, a parole report has to give evidence that some effort has gone into preparing it, and into working with the person concerned. Since we know very little about the ways in which parole decisions are made, it is unsafe to assume that a particular case is straightforward and therefore does not justify writing a full-scale report. Discussions with members of Local Review Committees have suggested to me that one of the large number of factors being judged (at an informal level) is the quality of work being undertaken by both field and prison probation teams with prisoners. A shoddy report will attract little respect.

Where purposeful work has occurred, report writers should take credit, indicating that a relationship has been built up. This adds credibility to any recommendation for release under supervision - not least because the writer is effectively agreeing to supervise the prisoner if parole is granted.

There are serious problems about confidentiality with reports for parole, in two senses. First, there is the difficulty that according to some of the people involved, such reports are actually confidential from their subjects. As indicated above, this is a surmountable obstacle. There may also be concern about the status of some of the information given by third parties: for example, if a spouse says, in the course of parole inquiries, that the prisoner will not be returning to live with them - but the prisoner has not been told of the decision. But in other cases, prejudicial information may be given by third parties who do not want the prisoner to know what they have said, and this is a very delicate situation. For example, allegations might be made about the inmate's behaviour towards a partner's children in the past. More time would be needed to deal with such circumstances.

The term 'home circumstances report' is really a misnomer, and we do not do clients justice if we take it literally. As is clear from those prisons which give detailed guidance about what they seek from parole reports, much more is needed: an assessment of the inmate, the likelihood of reoffending on parole in the light of home and other circumstances, and the prospect of supervision on release.

Finally, as with all social reports, it is necessary to bear in mind that there is almost no restriction on who has access to any reports on a prisoner's file. This may cause inmates considerable discomfort, and they should be in a position to decide whether or not certain information should form part of their case for parole: in short, are they prepared to risk confidential information for the chance of parole?. This is not to suggest that prison officers routinely behave unprofessionally with confidential information. But it is a real concern to many prisoners, and they have the right to know that no absolute guarantee can be given as to the confidentiality of material discussed in the course of preparing reports.

Unlike a court report, which is expected for a particular hearing, a parole report forms part of a dossier which is not dealt with until it is complete. While it would be unwise to obtain a reputation as someone whose reports are always late, it can be useful to negotiate with the institution's parole clerk in cases where there are good reasons for delay.

PLANNING FOR RELEASE

It is when we come to discuss with prisoners their plans for release that we are most likely to be able to make use of some of the theoretical material referred to in Chapter Two. An understanding of issues such as prisoners' changed awareness of time, their fears of, and the actual effects of institutionalisation can be most helpful both in showing that one has some understanding of the problems that they face and in devising appropriate ways of dealing with them.

Frequent references are made in the literature of social work with prisoners to the need to maintain links with the outside world. In fact, those who work from outside the prison are not well placed to assist with this. Ministers of religion, field probation officers and probation volunteers can help maintain links with the home town and with friends and loved ones, but only the prison authorities can decide to allow home leave, which is far more effective than visits or telephone calls in getting a prisoner to start planning for release. That being said, the probation service could work more purposefully than it has been in many areas in setting up pre-release groups that command the support of those who make decisions about home leave, and in requesting short home leaves. The difficulty is that every day is very similar in prison, and it is hard for people who have deliberately geared themselves not to think about release suddenly to reverse this self-protective attitude. In many cases, inmates have had to steel themselves not to think about long-delayed parole decisions (for some years, such decisions have routinely been announced months after the date when the prisoner would have been released had parole been granted, or only just before it, despite occasional injections of resources into the Home Office department concerned). Thus, Walter Probyn wrote:

without any warning, I was called before the governor, who was obviously overjoyed to inform me that I had been granted parole and would be leaving his prison in three weeks. I was apparently expected to leap with joy, but instead I felt a cold anger. They had destroyed everything significant in my life. During five previous parole reviews, they had destroyed the goodwill that existed for me in the outside world. On the five previous occasions, I had the promise of employment. I had all the favourable criteria that could have ensured my success on parole. Yet now, when I had no job to go to and now I had lost the support of people who felt the authorities had destroyed my good intentions, they decided to release me. Having done everything they could to prepare me for failure, they release me (Probyn, 1977).

So we should have no illusions about preparing people for release: it is far from easy.

Where clients have been able to maintain links with their families, relationships may well have changed during their time inside. At best, people will adjust to these changes and perhaps some couples' relationships are actually strengthened, but for many prisoners the loss of former roles is hurtful and they may need considerable help in adjusting.

Towards the end of a sentence, it can be helpful to suggest to a prisoner's family that they make a positive effort to start involving the inmate in decision-making again. Any help they can be given in visiting more regularly will obviously assist this, and there may be a case for additional 'welfare' visits and home leave.

It can also be useful to take up opportunities to discuss prisoners daydreams and fantasies about what they will do when they are released. Are these plans shared by their contacts outside, and how realistic are they? It is easy enough to get clients to tell you what they'd like to do when they get out, but it can be very difficult to hold them to a discussion about whether these ideas are realistic, and it may be necessary to return to the subject in a letter or on a subsequent visit. Some of this work can begin when reports are being prepared.

Popular 'common-sense' discussion of imprisonment often involves the assertion that prison must be too soft, otherwise people would not keep being sent back inside. Regardless of the merits of this argument, it is undeniably true that a very high proportion of prisoners do return. Paradoxically, this knowledge contributes to the fear of release in some cases: how are they to know that they will not be back? What is there for them on the outside? This anxiety is reflected in the quotation from Probyn above. There may be other reasons to fear release: the expectation of pressure from co-defendants or the police, for example. While people in the caring professions can do very little of practical value to help with such concerns, they can at least create an atmosphere that facilitates discussion, and help clients examine strategies for dealing with problems.

If the prisoner has avoided anything other than superficial contact with other people during the sentence, for any of the reasons outlined in Chapter Two, there may be real anxiety about social survival. We know that prisoners are likely to have been depressed for much of their time inside, and their experience may not suggest great grounds for optimism about release. If they have lived in fear for much of their sentence, or have chosen for other reasons to go through the process Abbott called 'hardening ourselves' (Abbott, 1982), it can be very difficult suddenly to put these protective devices into reverse. Once again, they may need help in explaining themselves to their loved ones.

Even those who seem to adapt well still tend to have disturbed sleep, waking early in the morning, and an initial uneasiness in open spaces and near loud traffic noise. Given the sanitary conditions in most British prisons, it is also hardly surprising that digestive problems persist at least for a while after release. There is almost certain to be some initial confusion about the management of time (see 'Loss of Structure', in Chapter Two), and it takes a while for released prisoners to adjust to making decisions about the use of their time again. This is easier, of course, if there is something to look forward to.

Where possible, opportunities need to be created for continuation of any positive experiences that may have occurred during the prisoner's sentence. In a minority of cases, inmates have been able to train in a skill, begin a educational course, work on bodybuilding, pursue some other leisure interest or an interest in religion, and it may be worth trying to set up ways of continuing with such pursuits. Experience suggests, however, there is little point in going to the trouble if the response is likely to be unenthusiastic.

Basic needs must be met on release, and the caring professions fall down in this respect from time to time. Last-minute checks need to be made to ensure that clients' accommodation arrangements still stand, and they need an early opportunity to claim benefits or receive an emergency loan if there are delays. Again, such requests are more likely to be forthcoming if a trusting relationship has been built up, and if you are going to be away from your office around the time of release, it helps to discuss other arrangements.

It is not worthwhile trying to involve the employment services in work with prisoners prior to their release, (except in the case of 'white-collar' workers, who may receive considerable assistance from the Apex Trust both during and after their sentences). Similarly, the Department of Social Security cannot process information about prisoners before their release, and although they receive a payment in lieu of their first week's benefit before they come out, there can still be problems in processing a fresh claim in the time available, especially in some inner-city areas. All this means that frequent contact should be offered (not imposed) during the first week or two after release.

Gaps in Existing Services.

Some kinds of prisoners seem to fare particularly badly under the existing arrangements, and this section will attempt to suggest some remedial actions open to the caring services.

CATEGORY A PRISONERS

There are special problems associated with being 'on the book'. Such prisoners (almost invariably male: the number of women Category A prisoners has been in single figures in recent years) are regarded as dangerous should they escape, and their movements are closely monitored. One consequence is that their visits are not necessarily held in private, and any telephone calls they make have to be in English, and made in the presence of a member of staff. They are only allowed visitors who have been approved by the Home Office, which uses a system of police vetting. This can be very disruptive in keeping up contacts with the outside world, especially for politically-motivated offenders whose friends may be regarded as undesirable.

An incidental effect of the provision of Category A places for women is that more than 30 other women prisoners are held in maximum security conditions which by most accounts are oppressive (see Chapter Two). There is some evidence that Durham H wing is used informally as a control measure against women who have been disruptive in other parts of the system. Its location in the North-East of England makes it a difficult place for many prisoners' visitors to get to.

Category A prisoners are particularly susceptible to the policy of sudden, unexpected moves from one prison to another, described in Chapter Two, under the provisions of Home Office Circular CI 10/1974. It is always worth checking that they are still where they were.

RULE 43

Under Prison Rule 43(1), prisoners can elect to be kept separately from others for their own protection. This raises issues for those working with them: Are they better off? How will they get back into normal conditions? What should they do if staff try to persuade them to come 'off the Rule'? Rule 43 can also be used by the prison authorities to segregate an individual for disciplinary reasons, and there is no legal right to make any representation about this (Herbert, 1990).

Generally speaking, it is assumed by other prisoners that everyone on Rule 43 is a 'nonce' (or 'nonsense case') - that is to say, a sexual offender. In fact, everyone knows that there are several other reasons for inmates being placed on Rule 43. It may relate to the nature of their offending: corrupt police and prison officers, if imprisoned, might choose separate confinement, as do 'super-grasses' and others whose offences cause popular revulsion.

The reasons can also arise from the behaviour of the individual: they may have made enemies (often connected with unpaid debts or informing).

Rule 43 prisoners are at the bottom of prison hierarchy. They may be made to feel in danger throughout their sentence, as this prisoner relates:

'The most despised nonces are the child molesters, and then there's a sort of graduation from there upwards. "You're fixed with that image: that's it, and you are despised. It's very hurtful. Then of course they try and take it out on you physically" '(Campbell, 1986).

He goes on to describe brutality at the hands of the police as well as other offenders. Other prisoners' accounts make it clear that prison officers collude with this (see for example Priestley, 1981, pp 33-4; Parker, 1969, p 178; O'Dwyer & Carlen, 1985, p 157) and spread information about individuals' offences in some prisons, which can lead to increased violence from the other prisoners who may understandably feel that such behaviour is officially sanctioned. This obviously has implications as to whether clients should be advised to go onto Rule 43, and it is hard for outsiders to know how safe conditions will be in particular prisons. Having said that, such incidents should be reported, and prison-based probation officers should be able to advise exactly what the conditions are in their institution.

It appears that prisoners' attitudes to sex offenders depend to some extent upon whether or not they are regarded as being fully responsible for their own actions - a worrying finding, in that it encourages people on Rule 43 to stick together and adopt a 'victim' role which reinforces their deviant identities (Taylor, 1972).

Because prisons are so overcrowded, the notion of Rule 43 as segregation no longer applies in most places. Apart from special regional units for prisoners on the Rule, conditions for such inmates are likely to be broadly similar to those of other prisoners, but separated on a wing or landing basis. In these conditions, a feeling of relative safety may be all that individuals have to gain from going on Rule 43, and they may be pressured by prison staff to return to normal location.

It is widely alleged that some sexual offenders on Rule 43 spend their time talking about the details of their offences and victims, and even circulating court depositions for use as pornography. As one writer about rapists points out, 'as long as a sex offender retains documented information about the victim, over which she has no control, she remains his victim' (Sabor, 1990), and a campaign has begun to restrict access to court documents of this kind.

The atmosphere among segregated prisoners is hardly conducive to the rehabilitation of individuals. Stigmatised people, cooped up together in close proximity and in fear, do not usually work on self-improvement, and in the prison setting, they are not given much help or incentive to examine their offending in a positive way. Indeed, it can be dangerous for them to identify themselves as undertaking group work aimed at tackling their offending patterns.

It has been suggested that most paedophiles do not regard their offending as wrong, and grouping large numbers of such offenders together is unlikely to lead to this belief being seriously challenged: imprisonment may reinforce the offending behaviour, according to some experienced police officers involved in investigation of child sexual abuse (see for example Sharrock, 1990).

In some prisons, however, psychologists, probation officers and chaplains do provide opportunities for group and individual work on offending behaviour, and once again, liaison is important to ensure that everyone is pulling in the same direction (Cowburn, 1989). Effective work by people from outside the prison to address offending behaviour is likely to need to be backed up by someone inside who can help the client to 'pick up the pieces' after painful discussions, and visits for such discussions need to be pre-planned with private facilities made available.

While prisoners on Rule 43 theoretically have the same rights and privileges as the remaining majority, conditions can be very much worse for them, and in particular their regime is likely to lack the normal stimuli of association and work, due to difficulties in providing staff cover to avoid incidents of violence against them. There may sometimes also be restrictions on visits. This clearly makes visits and letters from people outside more important for them than for other prisoners.

WOMEN IN PRISON

Consideration of all the ways in which women are differentially and less well treated in prison than men deserves a book on its own, and indeed there are several available (see for example Carlen et al, 1985; Bardsley, 1987; Casale, 1989; Carlen, 1990). This section is intended only to alert readers to the essential differences in regimes between men's and women's prisons and the recommended reading will point towards ways of exploring the issues further.

From their first contact with the penal system, women are disadvantaged. Disproportionate numbers of women are remanded in custody, for less serious offences than men. Of the 3,262 women and girls remanded in custody in 1987, 53% did not receive a custodial sentence on their return to the court (NACRO, 1989). Of those women imprisoned for the first time, 16% had no previous convictions (NCCL,1991). Unlike men, women offenders are frequently remanded in custody for medical reports when the eventual outcome is unlikely to be a custodial sentence (Morris, 1987) and they are even imprisoned more frequently if courts believe them to have failed as mothers (Carlen, 1983).

Only just over a quarter of the places in the women's prison system are in open prisons, and these are under-used, despite some overcrowding in secure establishments (Casale, 1989).

Women prisoners are far more likely to be treated as though they had psychological problems (Mandaraka-Sheppard, 1986; Dobash et al, 1986; Allen, 1987). Potent psychotropic drugs are given out in very large quantities, and some observers regard this as a deliberate control strategy (Carlen et al, 1985; Padel & Stevenson, 1988) combined with the ready availability of illicit drugs (Casale, 1989). The common belief in the nineteenth century that women would suffer the pains of imprisonment more acutely than men was used to justify the psychiatrisation of women's prisons during the 1960's.

In addition, women are consistently more than twice as likely to receive psychiatric sentencing disposals (including special hospital placement), which is a far higher difference than the comparative rates of mental illness would indicate (Allen, 1987).

Prison autobiographies show that women are subjected to far more stringent and petty restrictions than their male counterparts. Regimes are designed to produce a school-like atmosphere, but punishment can be severe. Josie O'Dwyer gives an absurd example:

she lost ten days' privileges for 'encouraging vermin' by feeding a squirrel (O'Dwyer & Carlen, 1985) but she goes on to describe a chilling informal use of solitary confinement. Women prisoners are formally punished more than twice as often as men (Padel & Stevenson, 1988).

Black women suffer double discrimination. There is a considerable over-representation of black women in the prisons. For example, 5% of the female population in 1986 was Afro-Caribbean, but 18% of the population of women's prisons. (Padel & Stevenson, 1988). This situation is getting worse each year: the 1987 figures showed that 23% of the women serving sentences were from black communities, and the same proportion of those on remand (as against 14% and 15% of male prisoners respectively: NACRO, 1989).

A high proportion of women prisoners (20-25% of the population at Holloway, for example) are of African or South American origin, serving long sentences for drug importation. These women tend to lose contact with their families, and have only recently been brought into the arrangements for parole and home leave in cases where the courts recommended deportation. In many cases, nobody explains their rights to them. As with male overseas prisoners, many of the foreign drug offenders seem to slip through the net of the welfare services (see for example, Casale, 1989, p 72; Tarzi & Hedges, 1990).

This combination of discrimination against women means that community agencies must tighten their gatekeeping where women offenders are concerned, to prevent them being pushed up-tariff. Once women offenders are imprisoned, there is surely a case for positive discrimination to ensure that they receive a good service from all the agencies involved, from workers who are aware of the effects of negative discrimination and committed to helping them to obtain their rights.

BLACK PRISONERS

Although Chapter Two touches on some of the particular issues faced by black prisoners, they are reiterated below because, once again, we may need to remind ourselves of the importance of providing professional services to all client groups, not simply to those whose needs are most obvious to us. It is a characteristic of services set up by white people that they tend to be delivered in a 'colour blind' way: white staff sometimes feel that is enough to treat all clients and potential clients 'the same'. This can lead to indirect discrimination because the differences between people and their needs are neglected.

Home Office Prison Department policy on race relations in prisons seems, on the face of things, quite liberal. But it is at best rhetorical, because the resources have not been made available to implement it, and no system of inspection seems capable of enforcing it. In practice, black prisoners are subjected to discriminatory attitudes by most prison staff, and nothing is done. For example, the Chief Inspector of Prisons noted when he visited Rudgate in 1988 that its race relations committee had never met and no monitoring was being done. Thus, when prison officers make assessments about individuals' suitability for parole, they can get away with making comments like this: 'Volatile, easily taken to make gestures typical of his ancestral background', and this: 'Like most of the group of inmates found guilty of drug smuggling and of Asian origin, he strongly denied guilt, claiming to have been set up' (quoted in NAPO, 1989/90).

These examples were reinforced by research in which 1255 prisoners' Standard Classification Forms were examined. The form asks prison officers to score prisoners' most likely attitude and behaviour. The analysis 'revealed that, whilst [Prison Department policies] have been largely successful in eliminating the use of derogatory language, it has proved more difficult to excise negative racial stereotypes from assessment [...] On every dimension more Asians received higher ratings than Whites, and more Whites received higher ratings than Blacks' (Genders & Player, 1989. The ethnic descriptions are those employed by the Home Office)

The same researchers found evidence that cell allocation was often arranged to avoid concentration of black prisoners, while white prisoners who made complaints about cell allocations on racist grounds were moved. Racial discrimination was still found in the allocation of inmate labour (although the Chief Inspector of Prisons said in his 1988 annual report that this appeared to have become less of a problem). Members of Boards of Visitors did not see it as part of their role to monitor the implementation of national policies on race issues. Race Relations Liaison Officers mostly do not publicise their responsibilities or invite complaints from inmates. Overall:

> This research suggests that racial discrimination is intrinsic to the social organization of prisons [...] when prison officers order their priorities, regardless of whether they are consciously expressed or unconsciously advanced, they draw upon clearly defined racial stereotypes, which systematically rationalize [...] the relative disadvantage of ethnic minorities (Genders & Player, 1989).

Substantial changes will be needed in society at large before the racism endemic in the criminal justice system, and particularly in the prisons, is in turn changed. As Paul Gordon puts it:

> The Director General of the prison service once spoke of an objective of the service being that of 'reflecting the spirit in which successive governments have made commitments to a multi-racial society'. Given that the reality of the British 'multi-racial society' is that of structured racism, persistent and widespread discrimination, and increasing harassment by forces of 'law and order', the prison service can be said to have achieved one of its two objectives (Gordon, 1983).

We cannot afford, however to throw up our hands in despair. Prisoners from black communities may seek protection from black and white professionals, and help in making complaints. They may want help in dealing with the extra stresses involved in imprisonment for them. They will demand both cultural awareness and anti-racist practice from agencies claiming to promote their welfare. It is the responsibility of white professionals to hold their agencies and the prison system to the rhetoric of their equal opportunities policies, and to expose breaches of these. This means that most of us have some more work to do in terms of making ourselves aware of what the issues are for black clients, and how we and our agencies should respond to the demands of black communities. Recent pronouncements by the management of the

Probation Service suggest that the rhetoric of equal opportunities is beginning to be fleshed out with some details of its practice implications: for example:

> ACOP believes that effective throughcare has to be preceded by positive contact in prison. It advises early allocation of black clients to a home probation officer; that adequate steps be taken to ensure that all reports to the institutions are scrutinised for racist statements; where there is evidence of written or oral racism these should be pursued with the prison authorities; that the black community is engaged, wherever possible, in throughcare (both in the prison and in the community) (ACOP, undated).

OVERSEAS PRISONERS

About 1,000 people are imprisoned under Britain's immigration laws every year. Unless they have committed criminal offences, they are treated as remand prisoners - which in many places means that they receive worse treatment than convicted prisoners. They often get little exercise, no access to legal advice, poor medical care, few opportunities to do anything constructive whilst inside, and no time to sort out their affairs in this country before being deported (D'Orey, 1984). This frequently means that women are deported along with children who have had little recent contact with them (although home leave has recently been introduced in cases where the Immigration Department is prepared to agree to it). The campaigning group, Women in Prison, is arguing for deportations to be delayed in cases where mothers need time to get to know their children again before taking them abroad with them. There are about 155 women in custody at any time who have been recommended for deportation, mostly serving sentences for drug offences (Heaven, 1990).

The policies of some of the helping agencies working with prisoners neglect to make any provision for prisoners from overseas, although each prison is meant to appoint a Deportation Liaison Officer. With some exceptions (for example, Inner London and West Midlands), Probation Services fail to engage with foreign prisoners in any purposeful way, and in many areas there is a blanket policy of not allocating a probation officer to inmates who have been recommended for deportation. This adds to the other types of disadvantage suffered by prisoners from abroad.

Throughout the prison system, inmates whose first language is not English are relatively poorly provided for. Their religious needs are usually met, but there may be no interpreter available for prisoners to use to express any other needs, which in practice means that an isolated prisoner speaking a minority language has no way of making needs or grievances known (although a few Probation Services do now provide trained interpreters who accompany probation officers on prison visits, and this should increase following guidance from the Association of Chief Officers of Probation).

Some small initiatives have been taken: for example, Women in Prison runs a support group for Spanish-speaking deportees, and also maintains contact with many Nigerian women prisoners. The Immigration Aid Unit run by the Joint Council for the Welfare of Immigrants in Birmingham offers help to prisoners in the Midlands, but some cases are inevitably overlooked and the office has only two staff (although J C W I in London also deals with prisoners' cases). Home Office funding would be needed before this could be replicated to provide for work with other, smaller groups of people in prison whose first language is not English. There is, however, an information pack for prisoners produced in 16 different languages by the Inner London Probation Service (see Tarzi & Hedges, 1990). At present, letters not written in English are sent for translation, which can cause considerable delays.

The law as to whether, and in what circumstances, the Race Relations Act of 1976 applies in prison is unclear. The allocation of prison labour was ruled in 1987 to fall under it, and a prisoner was compensated for discrimination, but this decision does not have the force of a binding precedent because it was made in the County Court (Genders & Player, 1989). It would be very difficult for most overseas prisoners to invoke its protection under the present circumstances. Given the evidence that prison staff make decisions on the basis of crude racial stereotyping, it seems likely that there is a considerable problem of discrimination against foreign prisoners in all aspects of prison life. The Home Office's race relations policy is unclear, and has been criticised for being implicitly racist in advocating the dispersal of black and foreign prisoners, thus suggesting, like the government's immigration policies, that black people rather than racism are the problem.

AIDS IN PRISON

Because of problems with maintaining the confidentiality of prisoners' HIV status, word can get around very quickly that an inmate is HIV positive, and neither prisoner officers nor fellow prisoners will necessarily be sufficiently well-informed to make the distinction between someone who is well and HIV positive and someone who has AIDS. The confidentiality issue is very important:

> Confidentiality is a principle which underpins the work of all professionals. Most of the time it is a simple consideration but at the margins it becomes complex with often competing loyalties. HIV/AIDS presents new challenges to the concept but also shows how undisciplined we have sometimes become in existing situations (ACOP, 1989).

The precautions taken in many prisons are such ludicrous over-reaction to prisoners being diagnosed HIV positive that it is hardly surprising that other inmates and the non-medical staff are sceptical about the reassurances they are given. In some respects, the precautions themselves compromise prisoners' right to confidentiality about their medical status: the practice of labelling individuals (and marking their prison files) as subject to Viral Infectivity Restrictions (VIR) even on a 'need to know basis' has meant that 'in practice it seems that little confidentiality exists' (Prison Reform Trust, 1988), and the Woolf Report recommended substantial changes.

Detailed guidelines in confidentiality and the 'need to know' have been issued to the Probation Service, and they provide a good model (ACOP, 1989). There is no general 'need to know' anyone's HIV status . Although HIV test should be voluntary, the Prison

Officers' Association has alleged that at least one governor (at Wandsworth in London) segregates prisoners regarded as 'from high risk groups' in a special HIV unit until they 'agreed to the test' - a procedure which clearly breaches Home Office rules but which has been going on since 1985 (Carvel, 1990).

This is not the place to rehearse the medical facts about HIV and AIDS: suffice it to say that while the virus is more likely to spread in the conditions prevailing in British prisons than in the community at large, it is not easy to contract. Those at risk are people involved in penetrative sex, and in drug use where needles are shared. Contact with significant quantities of blood or other bodily fluids spilt by someone with AIDS might also involve a risk, but the virus does not survive easily outside the body, and normal precautions for dealing with such accidents should be sufficient. It is also possible that home-made tattoos are a risky practice, in that needles are re-used without being sterilised (Curran, 1987). (For a fuller and more precise summary, see for example Prison Reform Trust, 1988).

People with AIDS and the related conditions need a stress-free environment to maintain their health, and with a good diet, enough sleep and regular exercise (Miller, 1987). This is unlikely to be available in prison under existing circumstances, particularly where medical officers are interpreting the VIR restrictions inflexibly. Few prisons allow normal association.

In many prisons this results in prisoners with HIV leading an extremely deprived existence with little to distract them from morbid contemplation of their situation. In terms of the risk of contagion there seems to be no advantage in segregating those known to have HIV from the general population. Clearly on normal location there are dangers of stigmatisation from other prisoners and staff, but this would not be so much of a problem if guidelines regarding confidentiality were adhered to (Prison Reform Trust, 1988).

There has even been a case of a leak of information about prisoner's seropositivity leading to a demonstration against his placement on normal location, and a prolonged and enforced time in the hospital wing followed. This has clear implications for the writers of court reports, in terms of confidentiality, but also for all professionals working with prisoners, in terms of educating themselves and their colleagues (ACOP, 1989).

As we have seen (in the section on prison psychologists in the previous chapter), people worried about whether they have AIDS need counselling about whether to take a test, and people testing seropositive need considerable support in dealing with the psychological consequences, including reactive depression. This can be managed and even turned to positive effect, by skilled helpers (Miller, 1987). Prison psychologists and others are receiving training in giving this sort of help, but the turnover of psychologists is so rapid that the necessary expertise is not always available. Some prisoners are still not receiving the counselling they need. A woman prisoner reported: 'the governor called me in and said I'd got it and that I should go back to work even though I was crying and all that. I thought I was dying' (McKeganey, 1990).

If the effect of being told of a positive test result are likely to include 'fear, anxiety, depression, shock, anger, guilt and bewilderment' (ACMD, 1988), how much more severe are these reactions likely to be in a prison environment, particularly when the prisoner is not usually afforded special facilities such as privacy or extra visits to discuss the test result with a partner, family or friends or to use the helplines and information services available to people outside prison (Prison Reform Trust, 1988).

Prisoners need additional support. After experimental routine testing for the virus in Ireland, there was a spate of suicides by inmates who had received test results, and a number of people have committed suicide outside prisons in the UK after receiving results (Richards, 1986).

Increasingly, medical officers and psychologists advise prisoners that taking a test in unlikely to have any advantages for them. People with AIDS have suggested that as far as test results are concerned, people should not be given this news if an appointment with a psychologist cannot be arranged until after a weekend - the first 72 hours are the worst (Richards, 1986).

The information available from prison medical officers may not always be adequate: in rural areas, they will be part-time local general practitioners whose knowledge may be limited (Prison Reform Trust, 1988). Although access to prisons by voluntary bodies with expertise in AIDS counselling has increased considerably in recent years, there are still problems funding this work.

Information about AIDS in prisons is being suppressed for political reasons, according to some observers. Research about the prevalence of high risk activities in prisons has been refused funding and 'The Home Office appears to take the position because sexual activity between prisoners and drug taking are forbidden such activity seldom occurs' (Thomas, 1990).

Combined with the fact that homosexual activity and drug use are in fact known about and condoned by ordinary prison staff, as an informal way of keeping the lid on in overcrowded prisons, this complacency becomes dangerous for individual prisoners who may not be fully aware of the risks because the information is not being systematically made available to them.

It has been established that up to 15,000 drug users are passing through British prisons each year (Fletcher, 1990) and heroin is freely available, though needles are less so (Pease, 1990). In the face of these problems, the Home Office reaction has been slow. Videos for staff and prisoners about the risks of AIDS (and attempting to dispel some of the myths) have been prepared by the Prison Medical Service in consultation with the voluntary organisations, and shown in most establishments. This material contains no information about condoms (which may have a failure rate of 15% if used for anal intercourse) because the Home Office continues to take the view that distributing condoms (or exchanging needles) would involve condoning illegal acts and might increase the incidence of homosexual acts and drug abuse. This is despite the fact that condoms are already provided for prisoners in Austria and Switzerland. Given the best estimates at the level at which high risk activities do take place, this is extreme complacency (see Thomas, 1990).

These facts raise a number of difficulties for those working with prisoners. It may be helpful to supply information from voluntary groups and health education sources where the prison has failed to do so, and where prisoners are known to be HIV positive, extra support should be given and, once again, additional effort made to ensure effective liaison between those working for the inmates' welfare. In the end, however, there are political decisions to be made before the situation will greatly improve. Matters are further complicated by many prisoners' distrust of the Prison Medical Service, which is seen as 'part of the system of discipline and control' (Fletcher, 1990). What caring professionals can do, however, is to ensure that they at least do not fall victim to the ignorance and prejudice which characterise so much of official dealings with people with HIV and AIDS.

LIFERS

On the face of it, it may seem strange to include lifers in a list of groups of prisoners who receive poor service: in some ways, they are treated as an elite. However, they are subject to particular rules and practices, with which some of the professionals involved are unfamiliar, and this can operate to their disadvantage. They also suffer disproportionately from the pains of imprisonment because of the indeterminacy of their sentences, and the problems associated with a parole system which operates in secret.

Some lifers know more about the system as it affects them than most probation officers. In one sense, this is not surprising: we all naturally take an extra interest in what affects us personally, and lifers have plenty of time to find out what they need to know. But they are a distinct group, and some of the professionals working with them receive little preparation for this work. There is a detailed set of instructions for prisons and probation staff about how to work with lifers(Home Office Circular 55/1984), but the attention of staff is not necessarily drawn to this, and many probation officers are unaware of its provisions. The Circular sets out the procedure whereby field probation officers supervising lifers will be backed up by a colleague who is familiar with the case, so that if something comes up and the supervising officer is not available, there is another person of whom enquiries can be made. Many officers are unaware of this and in many areas it is not followed.

How, it might be asked, does this disadvantage lifers? They have told researchers about the obvious inexperience of their probation officers with reference to the lifer system (for example see Coker & Martin, 1985, p 181; Williams, 1990, pp 237/8). Even where work with lifers is handled by specialist staff, prisoners' sense of powerlessness is likely to be increased if probation officers do not appear confident about the workings of the system.

In practice, lifers are visited on behalf of the Home Office by an experienced governor based there, who has considerable influence upon parole decisions, and there is no mechanism for probation officers to contact him.

Even where lifers were impressed with the commitment and performance of their probation officers, as many in the studies were, they felt that the implications and purpose of throughcare could have been better and more fully explained (Coker & Martin, 1985). There was a general feeling that lifers were not told what they needed to know. All bureaucracies ' normally ration services by manipulating the nature and quantity of the information made available about services' (Lipsky, 1980), and this is even more true in a total institution. Probation officers, whose professional ideology embraces the notion of openness with clients as the norm, nevertheless fail to tell lifers that they attend Lifer Review meetings partly to obtain information for use in parole reports, or what they do with the information they collect about clients serving life sentences. As Coker & Martin point out, this is a particular problem where prisoners may inadvertently give information which becomes prejudicial to their chances of parole:

> The English [sic] addiction to administrative secrecy is often at odds with the requirements of natural justice, and in the context of life imprisonment the challenge to secrecy is particularly important. Life sentence prisoners are in a specially vulnerable position, being almost entirely dependent upon the content of reports they never see. Those in charge of them need a fine sense of justice (Coker & Martin, 1985).

As they go on to point out, lifers are in a particularly unfortunate position when they have not been allowed to see court reports, which form a central part of the parole dossier. Although there is a legal right to be given a copy of the court report, lifers do not always recall having seen it. Some prisoners even feel that the reasons for involving probation officers with them are kept deliberately secret:

> you see, lifers don't get told how the system works, you just get told you've got an outside probation officer. You know, they go around saying, 'Well, yeah, but why?'; 'well, because you've got to have one.' 'But why?' and

> nobody'll tell 'em why. I mean, I've got through eight years, and nobody's really explained to me why I've got to have a probation officer.

Without labouring the point further, it does seem that some field probation officers lack clarity about their tasks with lifers, and that good practice does indeed involve openness and some clearing of the ground as to why officers are becoming involved, what powers they have and how they may be able to help. This would help avert some of the near-comical misunderstandings between probation officers anxious to offer counselling and lifers wanting practical help from people with common-sense (Coker & Martin, 1985, pp 184/6).

However clear the Probation Service is about its objectives in working with lifers, though, their feelings of being lost in a big and uncaring bureaucracy will persist while the parole process remains so secretive. An indeterminate sentence is particularly likely to be experienced as 'hard time'. For this reason, people working with lifers need to be particulary sensitive to the strategy of temporary withdrawal described in Chapter Two, and to discuss with the client the response that is expected at such times.

Similarly, we may need to admit that we do not know what is going on: some of the misunderstandings arise because of professionals' uneasiness about admitting how little power and influence they have, and yet most prisoners are well aware of this and appreciate straightforwardness and honesty.

5. Prisoners' Views: The Lessons of Research, and the Need for Change

The writings of ex-prisoners give a uniformly unenthusiastic picture of throughcare. Reasons range from a distaste for dependence upon stigmatising statutory services, and a wish to 'stand on their own feet', to outright anger at the treatment received from the relevant services in the past.

The overall lesson of the 'consumer perspective' of probation and other caring professionals' work with prisoners would seem to be that there is a need for greater clarity about what services are on offer and what they are meant to achieve, a need for greater honesty and openness between professionals and prisoners, and that where good relationships are made between prisoners and workers in the helping agencies on this basis, the generally poor perception of professionals working with prisoners does change. Enormous political and institutional changes are needed in the prison system, but individual workers can find ways of working within the system in good faith. The key to this would seem to be honesty about the limits of what can be achieved, and openness in going about this. Prisoners have very little choice about many aspects of their lives, including the processes of assessment for parole and judgments about their dangerousness. Genuineness in such work involves accepting this and not playing games. There is then a basis for helpful relationships between prisoners and professionals.

The evidence of research where prisoners were consulted is that they are well able to distinguish between structural failings of the helping services and personal commitment and authenticity on the part of individual workers. As Mike Fisher put it,

> Displaying greater sophistication than the researchers, some clients distinguish satisfaction with the way a service was given from satisfaction with the adequacy of the service itself [...] Indeed this distinction is a dominant theme throughout client studies in social work, reflecting

the crucial importance to the client of the relationship
within which services are provided (Fisher, 1983).

Similar findings are reported by Cohen (1971) and, referring
specifically to prisoners, by Corden et al (1980) and Williams
(1990; 1991). The traditional social work ideology that what
matters is the relationship between worker and client, however, is
not wholly vindicated by these researchers' work. The clients
clearly articulate their dissatisfactions about structural issues - lack
of resources (including workers' time), secrecy, delays,
paternalism. Research about prisoners' views shows that they
nevertheless value their relationship with an individual worker and
may base their decisions about future contact (including take-up of
voluntary after-care) upon it. The relationship does matter, but not
to the exclusion of the other issues. Thus, a prisoner discussing
parole reports said, 'The main thing is to build a relationship [...] If
they're doing reports, I do disagree with probation officers writing
reports on men they don't know: you've gotta know someone to
write a report on them'.

Another long-term prisoner said that if he'd had more regular
contact with a field probation officer, he'd have been more inclined
to ask for help with family problems. He did not anticipate having
contact with the Probation Service after his release, explaining, 'If
it did arise like, if I did need any help, which I don't think I would,
it's also what sort of relationship you've got with the fellow like.
At the moment, I don't know'.

Prisoners are already (at best) ambivalent about accepting the
offer of professional befriending, and we have to earn their trust.
The word 'relationship' is here being used in a commonsense way,
but the point relates too to the specialist, counselling sense of the
word: we cannot expect prisoners to trust us without putting in some
work first.

This makes how we work with prisoners all the more important.
If we disagree with (for example) the secrecy of the parole system,
why should we conceal this from our clients? If we reject the
paternalism of prison regimes, is it not better to say so, than to
collude with it? If we are in a position to expose the racism of the
system, and to protect the position of individuals victimised by it,
should we not do so? We shall sometimes find ourselves in conflict
with the system if we take up issues which are conventionally seen

as illegitimate, and one needs to pick carefully the issues on which to fight, but such a strategy has the merit of avoiding collusion with the prison system. It is a system which is in crisis precisely because it does not do what it claims to do; it does not reform people, it does not rehabilitate, and has trouble even incapacitating. The only part of its mission in which it is successful is in punishing offenders, and as we have seen, even there it fails because punishment is distributed in arbitrary and unjust ways.

The best that the caring professions can hope to achieve (apart from taking up these issues, and campaigning through bodies like unions, professional associations and single-issue campaigns) is to carry out our daily work with integrity and earn the respect of our clients. This book aims to give examples of what this means in practice when working with prisoners.

Ways Of Working Effectively With Prisoners: Summary Of Good Practice Points

(The following points are drawn from previous chapters, and this summary is intended only as a reminder, not as a checklist.)

To work effectively with prisoners, we need to

- familiarise ourselves with the accounts of prisoners' methods of coping with imprisonment. We need to be aware of their problems in dealing with the passage of time and their fears about changing during their sentences.

- find out the meaning of prison terminology, and be aware of the regimes in different prisons.

- find ways to 'interpret' prisoners' behaviour to their families and friends.

[SOME OF THE ABOVE CAN BE ACHIEVED BY ARRANGING A SHORT PLACEMENT WHICH ALLOWS US TO SPEND TIME WORKING ATTACHED TO A COLLEAGUE IN A PRISON]

- learn to treat prisoners as worthwhile individuals with positive potential. Like anyone else, they respond well to this.

- try to respect prisoners' individuality and autonomy, and work with them in ways which counteract the prison's tendency to infantilise them. We should be open with clients, and treat them as adults.

- find out whether prisoners have children, and help them to maintain links with them where appropriate.

- respect prisoners' wishes concerning contacts with families wherever possible, but consider offering to arrange support for spouses or families independent of referral by the prisoner.

- offer help in deciding what to tell the children about a parent's imprisonment.

- offer debt counselling where appropriate.

- create opportunities for the discussion of any changes in the balance of power in families, or any other changes brought on by imprisonment.

- respect prisoners' feelings of anger about their sentences, and learn not to raise false hopes (in the case of parole reports, applying this both to the prisoner and the family).

- respect the coping methods adopted by prisoners in a non-judgemental way (but point out the risks if necessary).

- create trusting relationships between ourselves and prisoners, but ensure that any limits on the confidentiality of the relationship are clearly understood.

- find ways of thinking critically and reflectively about our intervention (for example, in the case of probation officers, by constructive use of quarterly written summaries of our work and plans).

- be aware that depression is a reality for many prisoners.

- never deny that prisoners are suffering.

- remember that few things interest prisoners more than their rights. We need to keep up-to-date on such issues and, where appropriate, help inmates assert their rights.

- ensure that the needs of neglected groups such as deportees are not ignored.

- use the existing machinery to expose injustice, including racism and discrimination against women and Rule 43 prisoners.

- consider attending and contributing to institutional review meetings about prisoners.

- acknowledge, but not condone or collude with, the injustices and contradictions inherent in the prison system.

- avoid stereotyping prison officers. They are not all the same.

- accept that some prison visits are just for conversation. In the case of long-term prisoners, such visits are a step towards building up the relationship that may eventually lead to someone being released on parole.

- create opportunities to discuss offending, and feelings of guilt and grief.

- become familiar with, and be prepared to use, other sources of help for clients; chaplains, psychologists, probation volunteers, prison visitors, voluntary organisations offering specialist counselling (for example to people with AIDS), prison officers.

- maintain effective liaison with other caring professionals, and refer clients on to them in appropriate cases.

- recognise the importance of referrals made by colleagues based in prisons: prisoners may see them as more urgent than we do.

- consider the likely impact upon marginalised groups of clients before making changes in the system.

- make sure we plan our work so that we know prisoners reasonably well before writing reports that may affect their futures.

- treat all parole cases seriously. We should never assume that any application is an 'open and shut case': such an approach leads to the 'tick-sheet' mentality and the denial of opportunities.

- provide opportunities for prisoners to discuss their fears about release.

- check the local circumstances before giving people advice about electing to go onto Rule 43 isolation.

- prepare in advance for visits that may be difficult.

- be prepared to 'blow the whistle' on unacceptable behaviour, and offer support to the aggrieved party, be it a racist comment in a report, an attack on a client or disrespectful treatment of prisoners or colleagues on the basis of their gender or colour.

- be willing to subject ourselves to 'gatekeeping' processes, whereby our peers scrutinise our work with women, black people and labelled groups of offenders to ensure that our stereotypical assumptions are not leading to discrimination.

- accept and be open to criticism of our work.

- make bookings ourselves when visiting clients.

- be open to the contribution of voluntary and campaigning groups, who may be able to provide information and also direct help to individual prisoners.

- explain to clients how we like to work, and invite their reactions.

- be prepared to make brief visits where appropriate.

- prepare in advance, and check before breaking bad news to a prisoner.

- avoid giving false consolation.

- find out what we need to know before starting work with lifers.

- be aware of the changes people experience during long terms of imprisonment.

- give extra support to prisoners with AIDS.

- inform ourselves about drugs and sex in prison.

- perform what we promise to clients, particularly prisoners.

- be open to sharing our personal experiences with clients where appropriate.

- support prisoners in obtaining their rights to practise their religion - especially in the case of minorities whose rights are circumscribed or misunderstood.

- write some of our letters by hand, to give a personal touch.

- avoid sending routine, formal letters to prisoners, except when writing only to give notice of a planned visit.

- write to prisoners regularly.

- write clear, explicit letters which leave no room for misinterpretation or cause for anxiety.

- consider sending copies of important letters sent to prisoners to the prison probation team.

- visit prisoners on the basis of an agreed 'contract'.

Appendix - *Useful Organisations*

Apex Trust
Norfolk House, Smallbrook Queensway, Birmingham B5 4LJ Tel: 021-643 5666
Brixton Hill Place, London SW2 1HJ Tel: 081-671 7633
Helps tackle the employment problems of ex-prisoners and other ex-offenders through training, advice and support for individuals as well as striving to improve the employment climate in which they seek work.

Black Female Prisoners' Scheme
Brixton Enterprise Centre, 444 Brixton Road, London SW9 Tel: 071-733 5520
Advice and information for black women ex-prisoners. Visits to serving prisoners. Publicity on the particular discrimination faced by black criminalised women.

Clean Break Theatre Company, London Women's Centre, Wesley House, 4 Wild Court, London WC2B 5AU. Tel: 071-405 0765.
Touring company giving workshops for and performances by women ex-prisoners. Provides training in theatre skills and creative writing to women who have experience of confinement.

Help and Advice Line for Offenders' Wives
1 Printing House Street, Birmingham B4 6DE Tel: 021-236 8931
Advice and support for prisoners' families.

**National Association for the Care and Resettlement of Offenders
(NACRO)**, 169 Clapham Road, London SW9 0PU Tel: 071-582 6500
Free information service. Small cash grants to individual prisoners. Despite being largely government funded, also an effective campaigning organisation. Provides housing, employment, education/training and re-settlement services.

Prisoners' Advice and Information Network
(PAIN), BM-PAIN, London WC1N 3XX Tel: 071-542 3744
Umbrella group dealing with enquiries from prisoners and their families
and referring these to other organisations where appropriate.

Prison Reform Trust
59 Caledonian Road, London N1 9BU Tel: 071-278 9815
Campaigning group working on issues of prisoners' rights and the politics
of penal reform. Publishes the useful, informative and cheap Prison
Report (£5 per year, four issues), and distributes the Prisoners'
Information Pack, free to serving prisoners.

Prisoners' Families and Friends Service
51 Borough High Street, London SE1 1NB Tel: 071-403 4091
National advice service for prisoners' families.

PROP (National Prisoners' Movement)
BM-PROP, London WC1N 3XX Tel: 071 542 3744
Self-help campaigning group.

Scottish AIDS Monitor
PO Box 48, Edinburgh EH1 3SA Tel:; 031-557 3885
Care of Prisoners with AIDS, including a buddy scheme.

Scottish Association for the Care and Resettlement of Offenders
220 Renfrew Street, Glasgow G3 6TX Tel: 041-332 1763
53 George Street, Edinburgh EH2 2HT Tel: 031-226 4222
Advice and welfare for prisoners and their families; after care hostels,
employment schemes, travel schemes for visitors.

Terrence Higgins Trust
BM AIDS, London WC1N 3XX Tel: 071-833 2971
Advice and campaigning on AIDS.

Women in Prison
25 Horsell Road, London N5 1XL Tel: 071-609 7463
Publicises conditions for women in prison, assists individual prisoners
and campaigns for change.

Women in Special Hospitals and Secure Units
Address and phone number as for Women in Prison, with similar aims in
respect of women in special hospitals.

Women Prisoners' Resource Centre
Room I, 1 Thorpe Close, Ladbroke Grove, London W10 5XL Tel:
071-968 3121
Advice and information service to women prisoners and ex-prisoners;
help with resettlement. Provides information on women and criminal
justice to workers in the field. Distributes a comprehensive Reception
Pack to women prisoners.

Bibliography

NOTE: items marked with an asterisk are particularly recommended for further reading on the topic concerned

* Abbott, Jack Henry (1992), In the Belly of the Beast, Arrow.

Advisory Council on the Misuse of Drugs (1988), AIDS and Drug Misuse, HMSO.

Advisory Council on the Treatment of Offenders (1963), The Organisation of After-Care, Home Office, HMSO.

Alibhai, Yasmin, (1989), 'Colour bar', New Statesman and Society, 2, 53, pp 28-9.

* Allen, Hilary (1987), Justice Unbalanced: Gender, Psychiatry and Judicial Decisions, Open University Press.

Association of Chief Officers of Probation (1990), Position Statement on HIV, AIDS, Confidentiality and the Probation Service, ACOP.

Association of Chief Officers of Probation (1990), Position Statement on Principles of Throughcare Practice, ACOP.

Association of Chief Officers of Probation (undated), Anti-Racism Policy Statement, ACOP.

* Atherton, Richard (1987), Summons to Serve, Geoffrey Chapman.

Bardsley, Barney (1987), Flowers in Hell - An Investigation into Women and Crime, Pandora.

Bartell, John (1989), Chairman, Prison Officers' Association, personal correspondence with the author.

Barry, Nicola (1989), 'Serving Time on the Outside', Social Work Today, 29 June, p 23.

Bettelheim, Bruno (1972), Surviving and Other Essays, Thames & Hudson.

Birkinshaw, Patrick (1985), 'An Ombudsman for Prisoners', in Mike Maguire, Jon Vagg & Rod Morgan, (eds), Accountability and Prisons, Tavistock.

Blom-Cooper, Louis, (ed), (1974), Progress in Penal Reform, Clarendon Press, Oxford.

Bochel, Dorothy, (1976), Probation and After-Care: Its Development in England and Wales, Scottish Academic Press, Edinburgh.

Boseley, Sarah, (1990), 'Jail Death Man's Ward Bed Offer', The Guardian, 21 June.

Bottomley, A.K., & Liebling, A. (1989), 'Throughcare for Young Offenders in Custody', Prison Service Journal, April, pp 9-12.

Bowker, Lee, (1982), 'Victimizers and Victims in American Correctional Institutions', in Robert Johnson & Hans Toch, (eds), The Pains of Imprisonment, pp 63-76, Sage.

* Boyle, Jimmy, (1977), A Sense of Freedom, Pan.

Boyle, Jimmy, (1984), The Pain of Confinement, Pan.

Brodsky, S. L., (1975), Families and Friends of Men in Prison, Lexington, Massachusetts, Lexington Books.

Campbell, James, (1986), <u>Gate Fever: Voices from a Prison</u>, Weidenfeld & Nicolson.

* Carlen, Pat, (1983), <u>Women's Imprisonment: A Study of Social Control</u>, Routledge Kegan Paul.

* Carlen, Pat et al, (1985), <u>Criminal Women</u>, Polity.

* Carlen, Pat, (1990), <u>Alternatives to Women's Imprisonment</u>, Open University Press.

Carvel, John, (1991)'Prisoners Join Racism Debate', <u>The Guardian</u>, 7 March.

Carvel, John, (1990), 'HIV Unit Hunger Strike Ends', <u>The Guardian</u>, 7 June.

* Casale, Sylvia, (1989), <u>Women Inside</u>, Civil Liberties Trust.

Chaplin, B. G., Chairman, (1989), <u>Report of the Working Group on the Role of the Probation Service in Adult Establishments</u>, Home Office.

H M Chief Inspector of Prisons, (1989) <u>Report of Her Majesty's Chief Inspector of Prisons 1988</u>, HMSO.

Cohen, Alan, (1971), 'The Consumer's View: Retarded Mothers and the Social Services', <u>Social Work Today</u>, 1, pp 39-43.

* Cohen, Stanley & Taylor, Laurie, (1972), <u>Psychological Survival: the Experience of Long-term Imprisonment</u>, Penguin.

Cohen, Stanley & Taylor, Laurie, (1976), <u>Escape Attempts</u>, Allen Lane.

Cohen, Stanley & Taylor, Laurie, (1977), 'Talking About Prison Blues', in Bell, C. & Newby, H. (eds), <u>Doing Sociological Research</u>, Allen & Unwin, pp 67-86.

Cohen, Stanley & Taylor, Laurie, (undated, 1977 or 1978), Prison Secrets. Radical Alternatives to Prison, National Council for Civil Liberties.

Coggan, Geoff & Walker, Martin, (1982), Frightened for my Life: an Account of Deaths in British Prisons, Fontana.

* Coker, J. B. & Martin, J. P. (1985), Licensed to Live, Blackwell.

Corden, John et al, (1978), After Prison, Papers in Community Studies No 21, Department of Social Administration and Social Work, University of York.

Corden, John et al, (1979), 'Accommodation and Homelessness on Release from Prison', British Journal of Social Work, 9, 1, pp 75-86.

Corden, John et al, (1980) 'Prison Welfare and Voluntary After-Care', British Journal of Social Work, no 10, pp 71-86.

Corden, John & Clifton, Maggie, (1983), 'The Socially Isolated Prisoners Project', Research Bulletin, No 16, Home Office Research & Planning Unit, pp 45-8.

Cowburn, Malcolm, (1989), 'Pioneering Ways of Working with Male Sex Offenders', Community Care, 21 September.

Craig, Jean, (1984), The Probation Throughcare Services - a Report on a Consumer Survey, Policy, Planning & Research Unit Occasional Paper No 3, Stormont, Belfast.

Curran, Len, (1987), 'AIDS in prison', in McGurk et al, Applying Psychology to Imprisonment, HMSO, pp 341-60.

Davies, Martin, (1974), Prisoners of Society: Attitudes and After-care, Routledge Kegan Paul.

Dawtry, Frank, (1963), 'A New Look for After-care?', Justice of the Peace, no 127, 2 November, pp 702-4.

Dobash, Russell P. et al, (1986), The Imprisonment of Women, Basil Blackwell, Oxford.

* D'Orey, Stephanie, (1984), Immigration Prisoners. A Forgotten Minority, Runnymede Trust.

Evans, Rick et al, (1988), Prisoners' Welfare and Social Work Procedures: an Evaluation of the Shared Working Scheme at Stocken Prison. 1985-1988, D P S Report, Series 1, No 30, Home Office Prison Dept.

* Farber, M. (1944), 'Suffering and Time Perspective of the Prisoner', in Lewin, Kurt, (ed), Studies in Authority and Frustration, University of Iowa Press,

* Fisher, Mike, (1983), 'The Meaning of Client Satisfaction', in Fisher, Mike, (ed), Speaking of Clients, Social Services Monographs, Joint Unit for Social Services Research, University of Sheffield.

* Fitzgerald, Mike, (1977), Prisoners in Revolt, Penguin.

Fletcher, J. W. (1972), A Menace to Society, Elek.

* Fletcher, Harry, (1988), 'Black people and the Probation Service', NAPO News, October, pp 8/10.

Fletcher, Harry, (1990), 'Drug Use and Custody Crisis', NAPO News, May/June, pp 3/4.

Franey, Ros, (1989), 'The Lower Depths', New Statesman and Society, 10th November, pp 15-16.

* Genders, Elaine & Player, Elaine, (1989), Race Relations in Prisons, Clarendon, Oxford.

Gibbs, C. (1968), 'The Effects of Imprisonment of Women upon their Children', British Journal of Criminology, vol 11, pp 113-30.

* Goffman, Erving, (1968), Asylums, Penguin.

Goodstein, Lynne, (1982), 'A Quasi-Experimental Test of Prisoner Reactions to Determinate and Indeterminate Sentencing', in Parisi, Nicolette, (ed), Coping with Imprisonment, Sage pp 127-46.

* Gordon, Paul, (1983), White Law - Racism in the Police, Courts and Prisons, Pluto.

Gostin, Larry & Staunton, Marie, (1985), 'The Case for Prison Standards: Conditions of Confinement, Segregation and Medical Treatment', in Maguire, Mike et al, (eds), Accountability and Prisons, Tavistock, pp 81-96.

* Grimsey, Ben, (1974), 'The Importance of Letters to Prisoners', Probation Journal, no 21, pp 85-6.

Gunn, J et al, (1978), Psychiatric Aspects of Imprisonment, Academic Press.

Hague, Lt. Cdr. A., (1969), 'Address to the After-Care Staff Conference at Blackpool on 16/11/1963', mimeo, quoted in R. J. W. Foren, An Investigation into the Origins and Development of Social Casework in Prisons, unpublished MA thesis, University of Bradford.

Harris, Dai & Haigh, Richard, (eds), (1990), AIDS: a Guide to the Law, Terrence Higgins Trust/Routledge.

Heaven, Olga, (1990), Women in Prison, speaking at the conference 'Alternatives to Women's Imprisonment', University of Keele, 24 April.

Heimler, Eugene, (1959), Night of the Mist, Bodley Head.

Herbert, Shiranikha, (1990), 'An Improper Use of Rule 43', The Guardian, Law Report, 5 June.

* Hercules, Trevor, (1989), Labelled a Black Villain, Fourth Estate.

Hermann, Hanus, (1974), 'A Prisoner's Perspective', in Blom-Cooper, Louis, (ed), Progress in Penal Reform, Clarendon, pp 209-20.

Hicks, Jenny & Carlen, Pat, (1985), 'Jenny: In a Criminal Business', in Carlen, Pat, (ed), Criminal Women, Policy

Hicks, John, (1986), 'Probation and Prisons -Issues of Orientation', in Probation: Engaging with Custody. Proceedings of a professional conference held on July 2nd-4th 1986 at the University of York, National Association of Probation Officers.

* Hollows, Ann & Wood, Chris, (1983), 'Social Work in Prisons', in Lishman, Joyce, (ed.), Research Highlights 5: Social Work with Adult Offenders, University of Aberdeen, Department of Social Work.

Home Office, (1988), Report on the Work of the Prison Service. April 1987 - March 1988, Cm 516, HMSO.

Home Office, (1990), Crime. Justice and Protecting the Public, Cm 965, HMSO.

Home Office, (1990), Supervision & Punishment in the Community, Cm 966, HMSO.

Home Office, (1990), Partnership in Dealing with Offenders in the Community, Discussion Paper.

Howard, A. & Scott, R. A. (1965), 'A Proposed Formula for the Analysis of Stress in the Human Organism', Behavioral Science, 10, pp 141-60.

Howe, David, (1986), Social Workers and their Practice in Welfare Bureaucracies, Aldershot, Gower.

Hudson, Barbara, (1987), Justice through Punishment, Macmillan.

Hughes, Everett C., (1958), Men and their Work, Glencoe, Illinois, Free Press.

Irving, C. & Priestley, P., (1970), The Prisoner's View of After-care, South Wales and Severn Valley Regional Report, NACRO.

Jarvis, Fred, (1972), Advise, Assist and Befriend, a History of the Probation and After Care Service, National Association of Probation Officers.

Jepson, Norman & Elliott, Ken, (1985), Shared Working between Prison and Probation Officers, Home Office Research & Planning Unit, HMSO.

Jepson, Norman & Elliott, Ken, (1986), 'A Study of Shared Working between Prison and Probation Officers', Prison Service Journal, July, pp 5-8.

Johnson, Robert & Toch, Hans, (eds), (1986), The Pains of Imprisonment, Sage.

King, Roy D. et al, (1980), The Future of the Prison System, Gower, Farnborough.

Kingston, Rosalie, (1979), 'Through-Care: the Client's Point of View', Probation Journal, June, pp 38-43.

* Lipsky, Martin, (1980), Street-level Bureaucracy - Dilemmas of the Individual in Public Services, New York, Russell Sage Foundation.

Lloyd, Charles, (1986), Response to SNOP, Cambridge University Institute of Criminology.

Lombardo, L. X., (1981), <u>Guards Imprisoned: Correctional Officers at Work</u>, New York, Elsevier.

Lowe, P., (1989), <u>Personal Officer Work in Feltham YOI</u>, DPS Report, Series II, no 170, Home Office Prison Dept.

Lowson, D. M. (1970), <u>City Lads in Borstal</u>, Liverpool University Press.

Macartney, W. F. R. (1936), <u>Walls have Mouths</u>, Gollancz.

Maguire, Mike, (1987), 'Lifers, Tariff and Dangerousness', <u>Prison Service Journal</u>, April, pp 13-18.

Mandaraka-Sheppard, A., (1986), <u>The Dynamics of Aggression in Women's Prisons in England</u>, Gower.

* Masham, Baroness, (1990), 'Disabled Access to the Gaols', <u>Prison Report</u> 11, Prison Reform Trust, June.

Mathiesen, Thomas, (1965), <u>The Defence of the Weak - a Sociological Study of a Norwegian Correctional Institution</u>, Tavistock/ISTD.

* Matthews, Jill, (1983), <u>Forgotten Victims: How Prison affects the Family</u>, NACRO.

* McCarthy, John, (1981), 'The Modern Prison', in Jones, Howard, (ed), <u>Society against Crime</u>, Penguin.

McDougall, Cynthia, (1980), <u>Prisoners' Problems as viewed by Prisoners and Probation Officers at Acklington Prison</u>, DPS Report, Series I, no 18, Home Office Prison Dept.

McDougall, Cynthia, (1984), '<u>Shared Welfare Work in Prisons - a Time for Reappraisal?</u>', unpublished paper, Psychology Dept., Acklington Prison.

* McGurk, B. J. et al, (eds), (1987), <u>Applying Psychology to Imprisonment</u>, HMSO.

McKeganey, Neil, (1990), 'Responding to Risk', <u>Community Care</u>, 8 March, pp 25-6.

Miles, Tim, (1990), 'British Courts face Censure over Rough Justice for Blacks', <u>The Observer</u>, 6 May, p 8.

Millard, D., (1989), 'Looking Backwards to the Future', <u>Probation Journal</u>, vol 36 no 1, March, pp 18-21.

Miller, David, (1987), <u>Living with AIDS and HIV</u>, Macmillan.

* Monger, Mark, (1967), <u>Casework in After-Care</u>, Butterworths.

Monger, Mark et al, (1981), <u>Throughcare with Prisoners' Families</u>, University of Nottingham Department of Social Administration and Social Work, undated.

Morris, Alison, (1987), <u>Women, Crime and Criminal Justice</u>, Basil Blackwell.

Morris, Pauline, (1964), 'After-care and the Prisoner's Family', <u>British Journal of Criminology</u>, vol 4 no 4, April, pp 347-53.

NACRO, (1989), 'Women and criminal justice', <u>NACRO Briefing 91</u>.

NACRO, (1989), 'The Prison Disciplinary System: Recent Developments', <u>NACRO Briefing 10</u>.

NAPO, (1986), <u>Probation: Engaging with Custody, Proceedings of a professional conference 2-4 July 1986 at York University</u>, NAPO.

NAPO, (1987), <u>Community-based Through-care: the Case for Withdrawal of Seconded Probation Officers from Prisons</u>, NAPO,

NAPO, (1988/1989), 'Black People and the Criminal Justice System', NAPO News, December/January, pp 8-10.

NAPO, (1990), 'Framework for partnership between voluntary organisations and probation staff', mimeo, NAPO.

NAPO, (1990), 'SGM rejects Home Office Changes', NAPO News, April, p 1 .

Nash, M. R., (1988), 'If it can Happen Here... Shared Working at Albany Prison', Prison Service Journal, January, pp 11-14.

National Council for Civil Liberties, (1991), 'Prisons: Numbers', Civil Liberty Agenda, No.1.

Neate, Polly, (1990), 'Beyond the Gates', Community Care, 7 June, pp 24-7.

* Nicholson, Rita & Cowburn, Malcolm, (1990), 'Offence-based Work with Long Sentence Sex Offenders', Probation Journal, March, pp 10-13.

* Norman, Frank, (1987), Bang to Rights, Hogarth Press.

* O'Dwyer, Josie & Carlen, Pat, (1985), 'Josie: Surviving Holloway ... and other Women's Prisons', in Carlen, Pat et al, (eds), Criminal Women, Polity, pp139-81.

* Padel, Una & Stevenson, Prue, (1988), Insiders, Virago.

Lord Pakenham, Chair, (1961), Pakenham/Thompson Committee, Problems of the Ex-Prisoner, NCSS.

Parisi, Nicolette, (ed), (1982), Coping with Imprisonment, Perspectives in Criminal Justice 3, Sage.

Parker, Tony, (1969), The Twisting Lane, Hutchinson.

Parker, Tony, (ed), (1973), The Man Inside, Michael Joseph.

Parris, K. C., (1968), 'Casework in a Prison Setting', Probation, vol 14 no 2, July, pp 36-40.

Pearce, W. H., (1969), Reintegration of the Offender into the Community: New Resources and New Perspectives, paper given at the Canadian Congress of Corrections, mimeo, Durham County Probation Service.

Pease, Ken, (1990), 'Beyond the Wall', New Statesman and Society, 13 April, p 16.

* Peckham, Audrey, (1985), A Woman in Custody, Fontana.

Pendleton, John, (1973), 'Throughcare with prisoners and their families in England', International Journal of Offender Therapy and Comparative Criminology, vol 17, pp 15-28.

Pithouse, Andrew, (1987), Social Work: The Social Organisation of an Invisible Trade, Aldershot, Gower.

Priestley, Philip, (1972), 'The Prison Welfare Officer - a Case of Role Strain', British Journal of Sociology, vol 23 no 2, June, pp 221-35.

* Priestley, Philip, (1981), Community of Scapegoats: the Segregation of Sex Offenders and Informers in Prison, Pergamon.

Priestley, Philip, (1989), Jail Journeys : the English Prison Experience 1918-1990, Routledge.

Prison Officers' Association, (1963), 'The role of the modern prison officer', Prison Officers' Magazine, November, pp 330-3.

* Prison Reform Trust, (1988), HIV, AIDS and Prisons, Prison Reform Trust.

Prison Reform Trust, (1989), Report of a Prison Reform Trust seminar on 'The Needs of Asian Prisoners' held at the CBI Conference Centre on the afternoon of 26 October, PRT, mimeo.

* Prison Reform Trust, (1989), Prisoners' Information Pack, Prison Reform Trust, (free to prisoners).

Prison Service Chaplaincy, (1988), Directory and Guide on Religious Practices in HM Prison Service, Prison Service Chaplaincy, Home Office.

Probyn, Wally, (1977), Angel Face, Allen & Unwin.

* Raban, Tony, (1987), 'Removed from the Community - Prisoners and the Probation Service', in Harding, John, (ed), Probation and the Community, Tavistock, pp 83-99.

Raynor, Peter, (1985), Social Work, Justice and Control, Oxford, Basil Blackwell.

Richards, Barry, (1978), 'The Experience of Long-term Imprisonment, an Exploratory Investigation', British Journal of Criminology, vol 18 no 2, April, pp 162-9.

Richards, Thomas, (1986), 'Don't tell me on a Friday', British Medical Journal, 292, 5 April, p 943.

Rose, David, (1991), 'Children to spend Day with Holloway Mums', The Observer, 13 January.

Sabor, Monika, (1990), 'Double Jeopardy: Protecting the Victim of Sexual Assault', Probation Journal, March, pp 14-17.

Sapsford, R. J., (1983), Life Sentence Prisoners: Reactions, Responses and Change, Milton Keynes, Open University Press.

* Scraton, Phil et al, (1991), <u>Prisons under Protest</u>, Milton Keynes, Open University Press.

* Serge, Victor, (1970), <u>Men in Prison</u>, Gollancz.

Sharrock, David, (1990), 'Jail makes Paedophiles Worse, says Yard Chief', <u>The Guardian</u>, 8 June.

Shaw, Margaret, (1974), <u>Social Work in Prison</u>, Home Office Research Unit, HMSO.

* Shaw, Roger, (1981), <u>Children of Imprisoned Fathers</u>, Hodder & Stoughton.

Shaw, Roger, (1984), 'Shared Social Work in a Local Prison - a Matter of Trust', <u>Prison Service Journal</u>, July, pp 4-10.

Stern, Vivien, (1987), <u>Bricks of Shame</u>, Penguin.

Stokes, Sewell, (1965), <u>Our Dear Delinquents: a Cautionary Tale for Penal Reformers</u>, Heinemann.

* Stone, Nigel, (1985), 'Prison-based Work', in Walker, Hilary & Beaumont, Bill, (eds), <u>Working with Offenders</u>, Macmillan, pp 48-65.

Sykes, Gresham M., (1971), <u>The Society of Captives</u>, Princeton, New Jersey, Princeton University Press.

Tarleton, Peter, (1990), Chaplaincy, HM Prison Lindholme; personal correspondence with the author.

Tarzi, Ayesha, (1987), <u>Essential Information Pack for Overseas Prisoners</u>, available in 16 languages, Inner London Probation Service.

* Tarzi, Ayesha & Hedges, John, (1990), <u>A Prison within a Prison: a Study of Foreign Prisoners</u>, Inner London Probation Service.

Taylor, Laurie, (1972), 'The Significance and Interpretation of Replies to Motivational Questions: the Case of Sex Offenders', Sociology 6, pp 23-39.

Thomas, J. E., (1965), 'After-Care and the Prison Officer', Prison Service Journal, vol 4 no 16, pp 18-21.

Thomas, J. E., (1972), The English Prison Officer since 1850, a Study in Conflict, Routledge Kegan Paul.

Thomas, Philip, A., (1990), 'HIV/AIDS in Prisons', Howard Journal, vol 29 no 1, February, pp 1-13.

Toch, Hans et al, (1989), Coping: Maladaptation in Prisons, Oxford, Transaction.

* Treverton-Jones, G. D., (1989), Imprisonment: the Legal Status and Rights of Prisoners, Sweet & Maxwell.

Vagg, Jon, (1985), 'Independent Inspection: the Role of the Boards of Visitors', in Maguire, Mike et al, (eds), Accountability and Prisons, Tavistock, pp 124-40.

Walker, Hilary & Beaumont, Bill, (eds), (1985), Working with Offenders, Macmillan.

* White, Sheila, (1989), 'Mothers in Custody and the Punishment of Children', Probation Journal, September, pp 106-9.

Whitehead, Philip, (1987),'SNOP and the Probation Service: Some Neglected Features', Justice of the Peace, vol 151, 20 June, pp 392-3.

* Wilde, Oscar, (1949), De Profundis, Methuen.

Williams, Brian, (1990), Probation Work with Long-term Prisoners in a Dispersal Prison, unpublished M Phil thesis, University of Leicester.

Williams, Brian (1991), 'Probation Contact with Long-term Prisoners', Probation Journal, vol 38 no 1, March,

Wiseman, Bernard, (1990), Personal communication with the author.

Woolf, Lord Justice & Tumim, Judge Stephen, (1991), Prison Disturbances April 1990 - Report of an Inquiry, Cmd 1456, HMSO, (the Woolf Report),

Zamble, E. & Porporino, F. J., (1988), Coping Behaviour and Adaptation in Prison Inmates, New York, Spriger-Verlag.

Index

ORDER FROM CHAOS : RESPONDING TO TRAUMATIC EVENTS

Marion Gibson

Foreword by Colin Murray Parkes, MD FRC Psych

"With a knowledge that is based on personal experience, common sense and wide reading Marion Gibson outlines the plans, the training and the techniques that can be used by members of the caring professions and by volunteer counsellors to bring order out of chaos..... Disasters cause some to lose and others to hide their heads. One is reminded of the notice which was distributed in London during the blitzkrieg - 'If an incendiary bomb falls near you, don't lose your head, put it in a bucket and cover it with sand.' Marion Gibson has provided us with a bucket of sand with which we can dampen down the flames of disaster. Thus armed we have less need to panic or to hide."

ESSENTIAL READING for all helpers such as members of the emergency services, police, social workers, hospital personnel, clergy, managers of all organisations involved in disaster-response, victims and their families.

This book outlines the dynamics of disasters in terms of the emotional needs of those affected and suggests how agencies can plan to respond to those needs both in the immediate aftermath of a crisis and in the long term. It draws on relevant theory, the experience of recent disasters and the knowledge of those who care for the disaster victims. The helping process involved following major disasters is discussed in relation to personal crisis which happen to people every day. These personal disasters receive less attention from the public but the distress caused and rehabilitation process are similar.

MARION GIBSON is a Principal Social Worker, South and East Belfast Community Unit, Eastern Health and Social Services Board, Northern Ireland. She has been directly involved in post trauma counselling for some years and was a member of the national working party on disasters which dealt with the emotional and social aftercare

Price £9.49 (incl 50p p&p)   ISBN 0 900102 88 8

See end of this book for order form

WORKING WITH DEMENTIA:
GUIDELINES FOR PROFESSIONALS

Mary Marshall (Editor)

Government legislation has profoundly altered our approach to the care of dementia. The substantial increase in the number of old people, and the complex problems this will bring, is the major challenge for health and social care in the nineties. **Essential reading** for those working with people with dementia and their carers, this book is written by and for all non-medical workers in the field. It provides a basic introduction to dementia, and the skills and techniques of its management. Many real examples illustrate the jargon-free text.

Readership: Social workers, psychologists, occupational therapists, residential care workers, nursing home staff, hospital staff, day care staff, home helps and sheltered housing wardens, of general interest to carers in the community.

Mary Marshall is the Director of the Dementia Services Development Centre at Stirling University and a national figure in the field. Professionals from many disciplines have contributed their experience to this book including social workers, residential care and nursing home staff, home helps, occupational therapists and day care staff.

Price £9.45 (inc 50p p&p)   ISBN 0 900102 75 6

Available from Venture Press
Also in major bookshops

See end of this book for order form

BLACK PERSPECTIVES IN SOCIAL WORK

Bandana Ahmad

"I was so pleased to see this book written by a Black woman whose commitment to Black communities and their concerns shines through every page....Bandana Ahmad's book makes a valuable contribution to the growing debate about what is good quality practice in a multi-racial community" *Community Care*

A valuable training aid, written from a Black professional perspective and informed by an understanding of the conflict between the 'caring' quality of the social work profession and the reality of racism. Black Perspectives in Social Work challenges controlling and disempowering aspects of social work and explores alternatives which are both practical and achievable. It presents 'anti-racist social work' as within the mainstream of social work theory and practice rather than as a peripheral phenomenon. It is illustrated by case studies and examples of good practice and contains check lists to monitor individual performance.

Published in association with the Race Equality Unit, National Institute for Social Work.

Price £9.45 (including p&p)   **ISBN 0 900 102 780**

Available from Venture Press.
Also in major bookshops.

<u>**See end of this book for order form**</u>

CHILD SEXUAL ABUSE : WHOSE PROBLEM?
Reflections from Cleveland

Sue Richardson and Heather Bacon (Eds), Hilary Cashman, Marjorie Dunn, Marietta Higgs, Annette Lamballe-Armstrong, Geoffrey Wyatt

This book

— **AIMS** to be inspirational for those working at the frontiers who feel overwhelmed or demoralised by the problem of child sexual abuse.

— **EXPLORES** controversial issues regarding diagnosis, intervention and treatment.

— **DESCRIBES** for the first time intervention on behalf of children at a pre-disclosure stage.

— **CONTRIBUTES** to the creation of an alternative climate within which to debate future policy, legislation and practice.

— **IS NOT** a re-examination of the Cleveland crisis but sets the record straight on myths which influence current practice. **UNIQUELY** it provides key data from within the Cleveland experience - 'real' as opposed to institutional truth.

This is the first publication devoted to an analysis of Cleveland from a professional perspective. The book's aims and child-centred approach ensure a wide appeal to all involved in the welfare of children. The historical significance of Cleveland in transforming the issue of child sexual abuse make this an essential text for both academic and skills-based training.

Price £8.95 (inc 50p p&p)   **ISBN 0 900 102 934**

Available from Venture Press
Also in major bookshops

See end of this book for order form

INTERPRETERS IN PUBLIC SERVICES
Phil Baker
with
Zahida Hussain and Jane Saunders

THE FIRST PRACTICAL GUIDE for policy makers and managers providing public services to a multi-lingual community, INTERPRETERS IN PUBLIC SERVICES is illustrated with many examples of how different public bodies are tackling the need for interpreting.

IT:

— includes Codes of Practice, sample record formats and discussion of the pros and cons of different forms of provision.

— draws together data from a wide variety of national and local sources to paint a compelling picture of continuing linguistic deprivation in Britain.

— makes the legal case for an implied duty to communicate which is being accepted by increasing numbers of public bodies.

— includes a chapter on practice in Community Relations Councils based on a unique survey which explores the potential contradictions between the Community Relations Councils' roles as service provider and as pressure group.

— gives a comprehensive review of the latest training possibilities for both community language interpreters and for those using their services.

— identifies gaps in social policy and administration courses, and post-qualification training, and suggests training approaches.

— identifies the next steps required in a process which is fast gaining its own momentum - the integration of interpreting provision as a basic element of services in multi-lingual areas.

Phil Baker is Head of Staff Development, Harlow Council. Zahida Hussain and Jane Saunders are trainers and consultants in equal opportunities.

Price £9.45 (incl. 50p p&p)   **ISBN 0 900102 79 9**

Available from Venture Press
Also in major bookshops

See end of this book for order form

HOME AND AWAY
Respite Care in the Community

Carol Robinson

ESSENTIAL READING for health and social services professionals, carers and families.

Family-based respite care is now recognised as a vital element of community care provision.

Dr Carol Robinson has written the first practical handbook for proffesionals, carers and families. Comprehensive and authoritative, it gives step-by-step advice on all aspects of establishing and running a respite care scheme, ranging from guidance on securing finance to more complex issues which may arise.

This highly readable guide sets respite care provision in its context by reflecting on the economic, social and legal perspectives. The result is an invaluable resource book.

The author is a Research Fellow at the North Fry Research Centre, University of Bristol. She has conducted extensive research into to respite care and is currently working on a respite care project for young people with learning difficulties, funded by the Department of Health.

Price £8.45 (inc. 50p p&p)   **ISBN 0 900102 810**

Available from Venture Press
Also in major bookshops

See end of this book for order form

SEARCH:
The Social Services consultancy and training Directory 1991/2

— The FIRST directory of independent experts working in the social services and related fields, SEARCH offers national and regional information as a service to agencies across the disciplines.

— Entries from more than 300 consultants, trainers, independent social workers and researchers.

— Indexed by over 60 areas of work.

— ESSENTIAL READING for all local authority, health service and voluntary sector managers, lawyers and all who may need staff care, counselling and advice on social care issues.

Price £19.00 (incl. 50p p&p)   **ISBN 0 900102 829**

Available from Venture Press
Also in major bookshops

See end of this book for order form

If you wish to order any Venture Press title please complete the form below and return it to:
Venture Press, 16 Kent Street, Birmingham B5 6RD

Please send me _____ copies of _____

_____

I enclose a cheque payable to BASW Trading Ltd for £_____

Name_____

Address_____

_____

Please debit my Access/VISA Card no: (delete as appropriate)_____

Expiry Date_____

Please attach cardholder's name and address if different from above.

Signature_____ Date_____
(Negotiable rates for bulk orders)

- -